SOCCER DRILLS AND GAMES

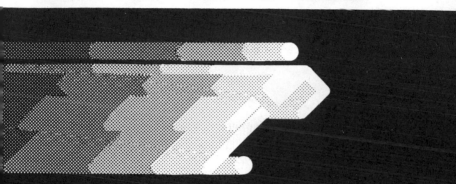

Techniques, strategies, and physical preparation

Written by **Günter Lammich**
Dr Heinz Kadow

Edited by **Gary N. Miller**
Technical Director
The Ontario Soccer Association

Sport Books Publisher Toronto

Translation by Linda Paul

Canadian Cataloguing in Publication Data

Lammich, Günter.
  Soccer drills and games

1st Canadian ed.
Translation of: Spiele Für das Fussballtraining.
ISBN 0-920905-10-2

1. Soccer – Training. I. Klavora, Peter.
II. Title.

GV943.L3513 1990 796.334 C86-095082-4

Distribution in Canada and worldwide by
Sport Books Publisher
278 Robert Street
Toronto, Ontario M5S 2K8

Printed in the United States

Contents

Y00₊5897

Foreword

Although not as popular as baseball, football, and hockey, soccer is becoming more and more popular in North America, especially among youth, boys and girls alike. But soccer is still a relatively new sport; therefore good literature on the subject is scarce. Most of what is available comes almost entirely from a few English-speaking countries. This book, in contrast, is a translation from German sports literature. It contains over one hundred practices and drills specifically designed for coaches and players at all levels of proficiency. They will discover much in the book that is both new and useful to the exercise and development of certain key game components. Each game is categorized in a systematic way for level of difficulty and necessary level of competence. Technical and tactical elements, physical conditioning, the exercise of creative thinking and game play, and the development of will power and determination are all given emphasis.

Editor

Introduction

The drills and games contained in this book — with a few exceptions — are based on the rules and regulations of the International Soccer Federation FIFA. Knowledge of these, therefore, is necessary for proper application of the games.

So that we do not have to thoroughly explain the rules in every game, and to keep the book uncomplicated, we have listed the most important points here.

1. The drills and games have been grouped according to their main purposes and have been systematized within each grouping — for example, one, two, and multiple-goal games — so as to aid the reader in recognizing the organizational and methodical characteristics of the game, as well as in understanding the objective of each game.

2. Comments are provided concerning such method as the application of a particular game to advanced players or its adaptability to play indoors. This commentary does not guarantee the game's suitability to particular teams or players. It illustrates, rather, the large variety of forms that the drills and games may take.

   A game's suitability for advanced performers may be determined according to the degree to which the game intensifies the training process: how it encourages the intensive development of physical conditioning and specific soccer skills.

3. Each drill has its own scoring and, as is usual in all competitive sport, the better or faster team emerges the winner. In the comparison drills and games, there is a "morale" rating, according to which the "better team" plays with the ball while the other must win the right to play again.

4. All standard rules relating to a player's equipment, to foul play, and unsportsmanlike behaviour, as well as regulations about the kick-off, the goal kick, the corner kick, the free kick, the penalty kick, the throw-in, and offside, are applicable and must be observed.

5. Any rules that vary with particular games — about the playing field set-up and limits, about the number of players, and about the duration of the game, have been included and explained in detail in the description of each game.

6. Deviations from the rules receive special mention. Finally, all games are illustrated by a diagram that contains the essentials of the game concept. However, these drawings are not always to scale. For a better overview, all the drills and games are numbered and arranged according to their main purpose.

An Overview of Drills and Games

Drills and Games for Warming Up (1-10) The drills and games in this group are characterized by general movement forms and are best suited for speeding up physical warm-up of the players. Attention must be paid to the fact that, although these games are to be practised intensively and without a break, players should not be stretched beyond their limits.

Drills and Games for Developing Fitness Abilities (11-44) These drills and games are designed particularly for developing in players high levels of endurance, speed, and agility. The methodology in drills and games developing endurance is based primarily on the various endurance training methods, extensive and intensive interval training methods, and pressure training methods (i.e., prolonged stress without a recovery phase). In each case, however — and this cannot be said often enough — the degree of stress must be adjusted to the ability of the player. In this, the timing and length of the necessary breaks have a special importance. In order to generate an effective endurance stimulus, it is necessary to practise until players are tired, to structure the rest period in such a way that a complete recovery is assured.

A different method is used for drills and games that develop speed and agility. Here sufficient time for recovery in the breaks should be allowed, since it is only in this way that the short periods of high stimulation have effect. The length of the breaks must be sufficient to allow an almost complete recovery of players.

Drills and Games for Teaching Technique (45-93) Learning soccer technique in drill and game forms has the advantage that sequences of movements must be carried out at a fast pace and under conditions similar to competition. A prerequisite, however, is that the players must already have mastered basic soccer techniques. These games are not suitable for learning the fundamental soccer skills; the beginner, using these drills and games, can easily get into the habit of making movement mistakes that can be corrected only with great difficulty.

The drills and games set high expectations in the use of the specific elements of technique: indeed, they exceed the demands of a normal soccer game. As a result, individual strengths and the ability to improvise are especially developed. Existing technique is greatly improved under the pressure of rapid play. Don't forget to encourage the training of both legs in these exercise games.

Drills and Games for Teaching Tactics (94-115) These drills and games teach not only individual but also collective tactics, and therefore demand intelligence and a good grasp of the game. When a tactical mistake occurs during the game, it is useful to interrupt and give corrective hints. However, room should be left for the individual capacity to improvise and create moments of surprise.

Drills and Games for Supplementary Training (116-124) While all the previously mentioned games are based on the soccer specific elements of technique and tactics, the supplementary drills and games are borrowed from other sports. They provide fun and relaxation in training and contribute to all-around fitness and performance development. The rules that govern them, however, have been simplified in part here in order to make their execution easier.

Symbols used in the illustrations

� Path of the player without the ball.
➤ Path of the player with the ball.
┅┅➤ Path of the ball.

Drills and Games
for Warming Up

5   Hitting Game

Number of Players Two teams with 6 to 8 players each.

Playing Field To the boundary lines of a lengthened penalty area.

Duration of Game Up to 20 min.

Objective of Game The players of one team attempt to pass the ball by deflecting it off an opponent. The other team tries to avoid being hit and tries to win the ball. A point is given for every hit.

Game Description Both teams are on the playing field. Only first-time passing is allowed. Dribbling is not allowed. The ball is given to the opposing side if it is missed or if it rolls over the boundary line, if it is touched first by the opponent after it has been passed, or if the player leaves the playing area. The player hit may only rejoin the game after the ball has first been touched by a teammate.

Variations The player hit must drop out; the game is over when one team has no players left.

Comments This game is particularly suitable for indoors, since little time is lost in retrieving the balls from out-of-bounds. It is also appropriate for advanced players.

6   Running Away From the Ball

Number of Players 10 to 12.

Playing Field Sideways across the soccer field.

Duration of Game Up to 20 min.

Objective of Game Two players pass the ball to each other and try to tag any of the other players with the ball below the hips. Any player who is hit must help catch the others. The game continues until only one player is left. Begin a new game.

Game Description The player with the ball may use first-time passes only. To better distinguish between the players with or without the ball, all players without the ball can begin wearing a coloured vest and take this off when they are tagged. Players who leave the playing area also count as tagged.

Variations All body parts of the player running away are targets.

Comments This game can be played indoors, where a barrier can be used. It is also suitable for advanced players.

7   Tigerball

Number of Players 4-on-1, 6-on-2, 8-on-3.

Playing Field Up to 20 m x 20 m.

Duration of Game Up to 20 min.

Objective of Game The players of the larger group pass the ball to each other, while the other player or players attempt to intercept the ball.

Game Description The player who touches the ball, trades places with the player who last passed it. The ball is also lost if it rolls over the boundary, falls to the ground (variant 3) or is not passed within the circle (variant 4). In this case, the player trades places with the one who was a defender. Handling the ball is not allowed even for the defender.

Variations 1. Specify the number of times the ball may be touched, or allow only first-time passing. 2. Play with two balls. In this case, a player also becomes a defender if he has passed a second ball to someone already in possession of a ball. 3. As a high ball game, the ball may not touch the ground. It can be juggled as

often as desired by one player. The timing of passing is left up to the player with the ball. 4. To teach kicking with the inside of the foot, all players form a circle with a 6 m radius and play the ball low across the circle to each other.

Comments Adjust the duration of play and the length of the recovery · breaks to suit the abilities of the players. The game is suitable for advanced players and may also be played indoors.

8   Stand-Go-Freeze

Number of Players 3 teams with 2 to 5 players each.

Playing Field Up to the boundary lines of a lengthened penalty area.

Duration of Game Up to 20 min.

Objective of Game Each player dribbles a ball. One team must tag the players of the other teams. Anyone who is tagged must sit down.

Game Description Tagging is done with the hand. Those who lose their balls or step over the boundary are also counted as tagged. These players must come back and sit down on the edge of the field. The tagged players are freed and allowed to play again when tagged by one of their own teammates. If one team has all of its players tagged, then another team becomes the catchers. The game is played until all teams have been caught once.

Variations 1. Anyone who is tagged must lie down (stomach or back) in order to make the freeing more difficult. 2. To free a player, only the ball may be touched when tagging.

Comments This game is suitable for playing on a soccer field or indoors.

9   Circle Tag

Number of Players 8 to 12 players.

Playing Field All but two of the players stand in a side-straddle position at a distance of 2 to 3 m from each other, forming a circle.

Duration of Game Up to 15 min.

Objective of Game Both the runner who breaks away and the catcher dribble balls outside the circle. If the runner is tagged by the catcher, the two trade places. If the runner passes the ball through the straddled legs of a player and creeps through before being tagged by the catcher, the player to whom the ball was passed replaces the catcher.

Game Description Running is only allowed outside the circle. Anyone who loses the ball or runs through the inner circle, becomes the catcher.

Variations 1. Rolling the ball with the hand. 2. Playing or dribbling the ball with the right or left foot, or right or left hand.

Comments The size of the circle should allow the catcher a chance to tag the runner. The game may be played indoors and is suitable for advanced players.

10 Changing Sides Tennis

Number of Players Up to 7 players.

Playing Field 18 m x 9 m, divided by a net 1 m high.

Duration of Game 20 x 30 min. or to 10 points.

Objective of Game In a rebound game, every player makes an effort to reach the ball passed to him, passing it back in such a way that the next player cannot pass the ball and must drop out. The last two players each receive a point.

Game Description An equal number of players form a row on each base line. One player begins by hitting the ball over the net with his foot (or knee), runs by the net on the right, and lines up as the last in the row of players standing there. Once the ball has touched the ground, the player standing first in line on the other side hits the ball back. He then changes to the other side. Anyone who fails to reach the ball, or misses, drops out.

Variations The stress is higher when extra exercises are required beside the net (such as push-ups, forward rolls, stretch jumps, etc.) or when, instead of running around the net, the player must jump over it.

Comments The game is suitable for advanced players.

Drills and Games for Developing Fitness Abilities

Drills and Games for Endurance

11   Fighting Through

Number of Players 1 to 2 groups of three and a regular goalkeeper.

Playing Field Half of a soccer field with a normal goal.

Duration of Game Up to 40 min. , by intervals: 5 min. play, 3 min. active recovery with easy technique exercises.

Objective of Game Each player fights for himself. As soon as he has the ball, the two other players of the group are his opponents. He must fight his way through in order to score a goal.

Game Description The game begins with a neutral kick-out by the goalkeeper. If a player loses the ball to another, the game continues with the player who lost the ball becoming a defender. If the ball goes out-of-bounds or a goal is scored, the goalkeeper gets the ball and the game begins again.

Variations 1. Two groups play at the same time in front of both goals. 2. At each 5-minute change, the teams are moved so that the best of one group plays against the best of one of the other groups.

Comments Adjust the duration of play and the length of the recovery breaks to suit the abilities of the players. The game is suitable for advanced players.

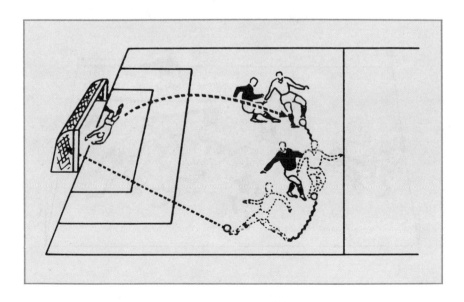

12 Game with a Moving Goal

Number of Players 10 players, 5-on-5.

Playing Field Half of the soccer field.

Duration of Game 5 x 5 min. with breaks for changing positions.

Objective of Game Both teams play into a moving goal that is marked by two players, one from each team. Each holds one end of a 2 m-long wood plank, and so forms the posts at the ends. This living goal must move in such a way that as few goals as possible are scored.

Game Description One team begins the game on the attack. To gain possession, the defender fights for the ball, or may gain possession when it goes out of bounds. After a goal is scored, the team whose player has won the ball plays on. Goals can be scored from both sides. The game is played intensively for 5 minutes, at which point the two players forming the living goal are replaced by two other players. Each player must be the goal once in the game. The players may not stand, sit, or lie down.

Variations The goal players make the goal smaller by walking bent over or in a duck walk.

13   Midfield Game

Number of Players 2 teams with 4 players each.

Playing Field 30 m x 20 m, on the touch lines are two small field goals whose openings face outward.

Duration of Game Played in intervals, up to 10 x 5 min.

Objective of Game Two players of one team must dribble the ball out of their own half of the field into that of the opponent in order to pass it to their forward, positioned in front of the goal. He is guarded by a fullback. .

Game Description A goal can only be scored after a pass from the opposing half. Crossing the playing field boundaries is not allowed. Passing from one's own half to the forward is punished, as is foul play, with a free kick. The game changes to the other side when the ball is lost. The two players playing in midfield change positions with the two positioned in front of the goals every 5 min.

Comments The length of the playing field, the duration of play in midfield, and the number of times the ball may be touched, can be changed according to the abilities of the players. Position change can take place after every goal. This game is suitable for advanced players. It can also be played indoors.

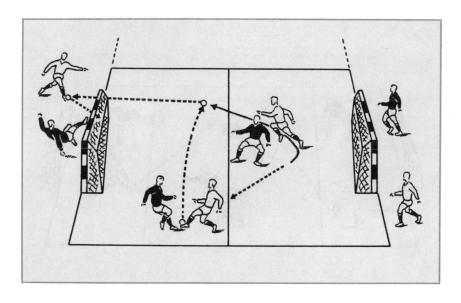

14   Fitness Game

Number of Players 2 teams of 5 players each.

Playing Field Lengthways, from penalty area to penalty area.

Duration of Game By intervals, up to 6 x 5 min.

Objective of Game Two players from each team are in their own penalty area, two are in midfield, and one is in the opponents' penalty area. The two players in midfield can score a point if they succeed in passing the ball to their teammate in the opponents' penalty area.

Game Description Two players begin in their own penalty area by attempting to outplay the opposing player and passing the ball to their teammates in midfield. In midfield, two play against two, and whoever has the ball can score a point. If the opponent wins the ball, the game changes without interruption to the other side.

Variations 1. Player change in midfield every 5 min. 2. A further point is scored if the single player in the penalty area can pass the ball back to his teammates in midfield.

Comments The game is simplified if only one member of each team is in the penalty area. The game is also suitable for advanced players.

15 Two-on-Two in the Corner

Number of Players 2 teams with 4 players each.

Playing Field Corner of a soccer field, approximately 15 m x 15 m.

Duration of Game 1 min. play, 1 min. recovery.

Objective of Game Each team must dribble with the ball over the opponents' line to score a goal. The winner is the team that has scored the most goals after a certain time.

Game Description Only two players of each team play at a time. They are relieved after 1 min. by two teammates. One team begins the game by attacking the opponents' goal line. With skillful teamwork it is possible to get into position so that the ball can be received and dribbled over the opponents' goal line. A goal is scored each time the ball is dribbled over the goal line.

Variations 1. The period of play is raised to 2 min. The recovery time must then also be lengthened and should be filled with technique exercises. 2. Rider soccer — two teams with 6 players each. 3-on-3, each with a partner on his back; 1 min. play, 1 min. recovery. Not suitable for school teams. 3. 3-on-3 in the penalty area. Two teams with 6 players each, from which only 3 play (the others take a rest); 5 x 2 min.

Comments This game is especially suited for advanced players. It can be played indoors.

16   Small-Field Soccer with a Hurdle Goal

Number of Players 2 teams with 5 to 7 players each.

Playing Field The halfway line and extended penalty line form the boundary lines; 3 m behind the "goal lines" are hurdle goals.

Duration of Game 4 to 6 x 5 min.

Objective of Game The team with the ball tries to score goals.

Game Description The game is played without a goalkeeper and without an offside. A goal is scored when the ball is shot through a hurdle. So that the hurdles cannot be blocked by a player standing directly in front of it, they are placed 3 m behind the goal line. The boundary lines may not be crossed by either the forward or the fullback, or a free kick is given from this spot.

Variations After each 5-min. interval, a 2 to 3 min. break may be added for technique exercises.

Comments The distance from the hurdles to the goal lines may be changed. The game is suitable for advanced players.

17   Endurance Game with Two Small Goals

Number of Players Three teams with 3 players each.

Playing Field Half of a soccer field, 2 small-field goals, 2 reserve balls.

Duration of Game Up to 3 x 5 min. for each team.

Objective of Game For 15 min. one team alternately attacks the two goals that are defended by the other two teams. Only after all rounds are played are the goals counted together and the winner declared.

Game Description The attacking team scores as many goals as it can in 15 min. The number of attacks depends on the amount of hard running by the players. After each lost ball, the game action changes to the other side. When a ball is shot, the attacking team immediately receives a reserve ball with which they continue playing. The game is played without offsides, corners, or throw-ins.

Variations 1. Increase in the duration of the play. 2. The number of players can be varied.

Comments The balls shot are collected while the other goal is being attacked. Also, the play must be adjusted to the abilities of the respective players. The game is suitable for advanced players.

18   Half Clearing

Number of Players 2 teams with 3 to 6 players each.

Playing Field Half of a soccer field, 2 small field goals, and a halfway line.

Duration of Game Up to 90 min.

Objective of Game All players of the attacking team must have cleared their field and be in the opponents' half to score a goal, while the other team defends its goal and tries to win the ball.

Game Description A goal is only valid if all players of the attacking team are in the opponents' half. The opponent gets the ball if not all the players have run over the halfway line during the goal shot, if they capture the ball, or when a throw-in, corner, or foul occurs. The game is played without a regular goalkeeper. The last player of each team in front of the goal may hit the ball with his hands. Offside is not used.

Variations 1. The attacking team keeps the ball and, after each goal, keeps playing. The game simply changes to the other side. 2. Goals are counted double if one or more players of the defending team are still in the opposing half.

Comments Teams with 7 to 11 players use the whole soccer field. If the game is played with goalkeepers, they do not need to clear their half. This game is suitable for players of all ages and levels of ability.

19   Game with Two Open Goals

Number of Players 2 teams with 2 to 4 players.

Playing Field Half of a soccer field, two goals, 2 m wide and 20 m apart, are marked with flags.

Duration of Game One team attacks to score goals; the other defends and tries to win the ball. Since goals are open, there is hardly any interruption in the game and both teams are forced to run without interruption.

Game Description A goal can be scored from either side of the flags. The height of the goal equals the height of the flags, so that balls flying over the goal are not allowed. Balls going out of bounds are thrown in. The game is played without a goalkeeper. Handling the ball, as well as running through the goal, is not allowed; the penalty is a 10 m free kick.

Comments The width of the goal may be reduced to 1 m for experienced players, or increased to 3 m for beginners. With a decrease in the distance between the goals, the game is suitable for indoors.

20   Game with Backwards Goals

Number of Players 2 teams with 4 to 6 players each.

Playing Field Half of soccer field, two small field goals, 20 m apart, facing towards the end lines.

Duration of Game Up to 90 min.

Objective of Game One team begins and attacks the opponents' goal to score, and if the ball is lost, tries to prevent scoring on its own goal.

Game Description The game begins with a kick-off on the halfway line. The game is played without a regular goalkeeper. The last player of each team in front of his own goal may handle the ball. The opponents receive the ball if they capture it, if the ball goes into the sidelines, after foul play, and after a goal.

Variations 1. In order to lengthen the running distances, set the goals 40 m apart. 2. The tempo is increased if the game is continued immediately after every goal.

Comments This game is suitable for players of all ages and abilities, providing the intensity of play is adjusted to accommodate various skill levels.

21 Mixed Game

Purpose Developing endurance in combination with acceleration speed, jumping ability, and mobility.

Number of Players 2 teams with 8 to 11 players each.

Playing Field Soccer field.

Object of Game The most important point of this game is the use of interruptions, which occur according to the rules of soccer, and are used for extra conditioning and as a form of punishment for players. For example, for every free kick awarded, all players of the team responsible must do a 10 m sprint and come back to take up their old positions. For every ball going into the sidelines the penalized players must perform various exercises (push-ups, sit-ups, etc) at great intensity. A series of jumps is demanded of each player for every corner kick. Only after the penalty exercises have been completed is the game continued.

Game Rule Points are awarded according to the rules of soccer

Variations It is possible to use all interruptions of the game for such forced conditioning, for example, kick-off, penalty kick, offside, and substitutions. Goals should be excluded from this, since all players find the extra running, exercising, and jumping to be very exhausting and will avoid anything that demands greater exertion.

Comments Strength exercises could replace running, depending on the athletic development and age of the team.

22. Playing Crossways

Purpose Teaching endurance.

Number of Players 4 teams with 3 to 5 players each.

Playing Field Soccer field containing 2 m wide goals set up with flag poles at every corner.

Duration of Game 4 x 20 to 30 min.

Object of Game Each team has a goal to defend and must attack the goal opposite its own in order to score. Because of the diagonal running paths, the players are forced to run more than usual. The endurance performance is also increased since the attacking team must clear its own half of the field. Since all four teams play crossways at the same time, higher demands are made on the observation abilities of the players.

Game Rule Two teams begin the game at the same time in their own half of the field and attack their opponents' goals. A goal can be scored only when all players of the attacking team have cleared their own half of the field and are in the opponents' half. In addition, the ball must have crossed the goal line at the height

of the flag poles. Handling the ball is not allowed.

The game is played without offside and corners. Balls going into the sidelines are kicked in at the spot where they crossed the line.

Variations Two teams and their scores may be combined. The winner is the team which, after adding up both results, has scored more goals than the opponent.

Comments In this game two referees are required. All four teams should have easily identifiable uniforms.

23 Diagonal Four Goal Game

Number of Players Two teams with 6 to 8 players each.

Playing Field Soccer field with a goal placed in the middle of each side line.

Duration of Game Up to 60 min.

Objective of Game The attacking team tries to score on either of the opponents' goals, and to defend its own goals if possession of the ball is lost.

Game Description A goal is scored when the ball goes over the line of one of the two diagonally opposite goals. It is up to the attacking team to decide which of the two goals to attack. Scoring opportunities are created by rapid game movement which allows shooters to get free. The opponent gains possession of the ball if it is captured, if it goes into the sidelines, or following foul play.

Variations 1. The number of times the ball may be touched is specified (as often as desired, first-time passing). 2. Play into 4 corners, half of the playing field in which 2 m-wide goals are set up in the corners with flagstaffs. The game is played without a goalkeeper.

Comments The fewer the players, the greater the stress. The game is suitable for advanced players.

24 Six-on-Six without a Goal

Number of Players 12 players, 6-on-6.

Playing Field Half of the soccer field.

Duration of Game Intervals of 5 min., up to 30 min.

Objective of Game Both teams try to keep the ball as long as possible. The tempo of the game can be speeded up by allowing only direct passes, without dribbling for 5-minute periods. Afterwards the game tempo should be slowed down again with the ball being played two or more times. A point is given for every pass.

Game Description One team begins the game and plays until it loses the ball. The opposing team gets the ball if they capture it, if the ball goes into the sidelines, or if the opponent touches it more than the allowed number of times. A referee is required to count the number of passes by each team.

Comments Begin by playing the ball several times, then increase the tempo by allowing the ball to be touched only twice. Only then should the coach demand first-time passing. Teams with strong performance records should play with relatively short breaks. Allow weaker teams to play with correspondingly longer breaks and on a smaller field.

25   Five-on-Three

Number of Players 8 players, 5-on-3.

Playing Field 30 m x 30 m.

Duration of Game Up to six 5 min. intervals.

Object of Game Both teams must try to hold onto the ball as long as possible. A point is awarded for each minute of possession. The winner is the team which, after a specified time, has earned the most points.

Game Description While the players of one team pass the ball to each other, the other team must try to win the ball. Each player on the five-man team is given a certain limitation; for example, they may only make first-time passes, while the three-man team is allowed to play freely using all techniques. If a team scores a point, it can maintain possession or give the ball to the opponent, depending on the agreement made.

Variations 1. The team with five players may only pass low or with the left leg. 2. After every five-minute interval, three players from the five-man team form a new three-man team.

Comments Adjust the stress to the abilities of the players. The game is suitable for advanced players.

Drills and Games for Speed

26   Handicap Game

Number of Players 6 to 10 players, at least 3-on-3, at most 5-on-5.

Playing Field Half of the soccer field with halfway line marked, goal areas chalked in, and 2 small field goals.

Duration of Game Up to 40 min.

Objective of Game One team attacks, the other defends the goal. The attackers stand on the halfway line, and receive the ball passed by an opponent from the opposite goal area. While the attackers try to exploit the favorable ratio and score a goal, the opponent sprints to the other side in order to complete his team.

Game Description After a goal is scored, or the ball is lost, the opponent receives the ball. The defenders become attackers. The other team now has the handicap and must defend the goal. Handling the ball is forbidden; offside is removed.

Variations Increase the sprinting distance by moving the goal.

Comments It is useful to have all players take turns at having the handicap. The game is suitable for advanced players.

27 Narrow Zone Game

Number of Players 2 teams of 3 players each.

Playing Field 70 m x 16.5 m (the penalty area extended to the side lines), a zone 8 m wide is marked at each end.

Duration of Game 2 x 10 min. to 2 x 20 min.

Objective of Game The attacking team tries to play the ball into the opponents' zone and to bring it under control. If the opponents have the ball, they defends their own zone.

Game Description One point is scored if the ball is kicked into the opponents' zone and a teammate retrieves it before it rolls over the outer boundary. The team's own zone may not be entered. Breaking the rules is penalized by an indirect free kick.

Variations 1. The size of the zone can be changed according to the abilities of the players. The better the players, the smaller the zone will be. 2. The whole playing field is divided by a halfway line. Points are given only for a pass from one half to the other.

Comments Since the stress in this game is quite high, active breaks should be incorporated. The game is suitable for advanced players.

28 Running Game with Three-Man Teams

Number of Players As many as desired, 3 players to a team.

Playing Field 50 m x 20 m, divided into a 30 m running field and a 20 m x 20 m target field; a post is set up in the running field, 20 m from from the side line.

Duration of Game Up to 30 min.

Objective of Game One player is in front of the starting line, and both of his opponents are in the target field. The player who kicks the ball from the starting line into the target field and then sprints around the running post and back to the starting line, without being tagged by the ball by one of his opponents, wins a point and a free ball.

Game Description The players receive the numbers 1, 2, and 3. Player 1 begins. If he succeeds in kicking the ball into the target field and in running around the post to the starting line without getting tagged by the ball, he is free. He receives a point and may start again. If he is tagged, player 2 takes over his position and player 1 must go into the target field. The same applies when the target kick does not land in the target field. Both opponents can run over to the target field line in order to throw the ball.

Comments Adjust the length and width of the fields, as well as the running distance to the abilities of the players.

29   Long Ball Game

Number of Players Two teams with 4 to 10 players each.

Playing Field Half of a soccer field with a flag in the middle of the marked halfway line.

Duration of Game Up to 20 starts.

Objective of Game Two teams stand across from each other on the touch lines. One team must kick the ball into the opponents' half and at the same moment run around the flag and back. The other team must catch the ball, and through good teamwork, tag as many opponents as possible.

Game Description For each player tagged, a point is awarded. The same applies if the ball does not reach the opponents' half at the beginning of the game or if a player does not run around the flag. The teams change their functions after every run. The winner is only declared after each player has begun the game once.

Variations The tagging team may only pass directly after passing.

Comments Adjust the size of the playing field and the number of runs to the abilities of the players.

30   Short Sprinting Game

Number of Players 3 players.

Playing Field Half of the soccer pitch.(The cut-off marks between the extended goal line and the penalty area must be exactly marked as starting points.)

Duration of Game Up to 30 min. or 20 starts.

Objective of Game Each player tries to capture the ball, dribble around his opponent, and score a goal.

Game Description One player is in goal, the other two are left and right of him on the starting points. The goalkeeper kicks the ball in the middle. After his goal kick, both partners sprint to the ball. The player who touches it first, receives a point.

A further point is given if the player succeeds in dribbling around his opponent and shooting a goal. After every goal, the game begins again.

Variations 1. Starts from various positions. 2. In case of significant differences in speed among players, use a corresponding handicap.

Comments The teaching of speed endurance is also possible with correspondingly short breaks.

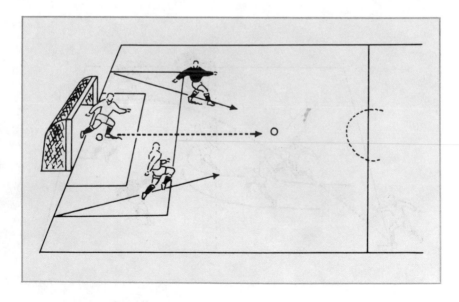

31   Group Sprinting Games

Number of Players 2 groups with 4 players each, and 2 goalkeepers.

Playing Field Soccer field with a marked central circle.

Duration of Game Up to 30 min. or up to 5 starts per player.

Objective of Game Four opposing pairs are set up. All players dribble a ball into the central circle. If a player is called, he sprints with the ball on his foot to the goal and attempts to score. His opponent runs after him without the ball and tries to defend the goal.

Game Description It makes no difference which goal the player who has been called out sprints to. If he loses the ball to his opponent, he begins the game again in the central circle. A player may only leave the central circle after he has been called. The ball changes owner and the player gets a 3 m lead if there is foul play.

Variations 1. A player may dribble farther up to the goal if he captures the ball. 2. The groups can alternate beginning the game independently without being called.

Comments All players must allowed the same number of sprints. Make up a starting list.

32   Fighting for The Ball

Number of Players 2 teams with 4 to 6 players each.

Playing Field 40 x 29 m with the halfway line marked.

Duration of Game Up to 20 starts.

Objective of Game Both teams stand on the narrow side of the playing field, across from each other. Two balls less than the number of players (6 balls for 8 players, 10 balls for 12 players, etc.) are lined up on the halfway line.

At a signal, both teams start for the middle to dribble as many balls as possible over their lines. A point is given for each ball.

Game Description The two players who do not get balls try to kick as many balls as possible away from the opponent. Balls that are kicked over the touch line are lost. Balls that are dribbled over the team's own line are won, and are given one point each. It is important that the player dribbles the ball over the line with his foot. Balls that are kicked over are invalid.

Variations Specify the method of dribbling.

Comments It is useful to have two referees each one looking after one half of the playing field.

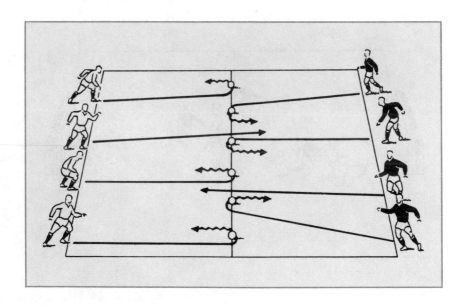

33   Chinese Soccer Tennis

Number of Players 4 players, 2-on-2.

Playing Field 16 x 16 m, divided through the middle into 2 fields by a 1 m high net.

Duration of Game 2 winning sets up to 21 points.

Objective of Game The ball must be kicked over the net into the opponents' half. The player who kicks the ball changes his field.

Game Description The game begins with the serve behind the playing field boundary. The ball must bounce once in the opposing field and may not be touched more than once. The serve changes to the opponent and he receives a point after every mistake. An error has been committed if the ball is touched by a player who has not yet changed fields, if it bounces more than once or is played with first-time passes, if it touches the net during the serve or lands outside the boundary, or if it is touched with the hands or more than once.

Variations 1. Technically weaker teams may allow the ball to bounce more than once. 2. Go over obstacles set up at the sides.

Comments The game can be played indoors.

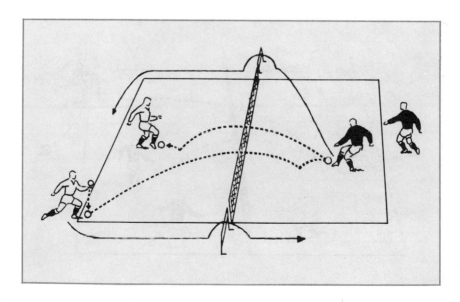

34　Soccer Tennis with Relay Posts

Number of Players 6 players, 3-on-3.

Playing Field 20 x 24, divided through the middle by a 1 m high net (a rope or a row of hurdles will do just as well). 3 m behind each playing field boundary is a post (box cover, medicine ball, or something similar) that must be hit.

Duration of Game 2 winning sets to 21 points. If each team wins a set, a tie-breaker is necessary, during which sides must be changed after 10 points.

Objective of Game After he has kicked the ball into the opponents' half, the player runs as fast as he can to the post and back.

Game Description The game begins with a serve behind the team's own playing field boundary. The player's ability in certain kicking methods is demanded for the serve. The ball can be hit from the ground — as a drop kick, and from the air. Specify the leg that players must use to kick the ball. The ball must bounce once in the opponents' field before it may be kicked back. The serve follows and changes after each mistake. The opposing team receives a point with each mistake. An error is committed when the ball:

1. is kicked back by a player who was near the ball but had not yet touched the post;

2. bounces more than once or is played directly;

3. touches the net or lands outside the boundary during the serve;

4. is hit with the hand or more than once; or

5. if a player steps over the opponents' boundary.

Variations 1. Touch the post with the left or right hand, with a foot or with the buttocks. 2. If the game action with especially good players becomes so fast that it is an effort for the players to reach their field again, then each opposing player must touch the ball once before it is kicked back.

Comments The distance of the post from the boundary of the playing field is dependent on the abilities of the teams. In addition, it is possible to set up two more on the touch lines, so that the player can decide which post to hit, and the bothersome running back and forth in one's own field can be kept to a minimum. The game may be played indoors.

35 Post Relay Game

Number of Players As many as desired, 2 equal teams.

Playing Field Starting line with 2 posts marked by flag staffs or medicine balls 20 to 30 m away.

Duration of Game Up to 20 min. or to 10 heats for each team.

Objective of Game The players of each team try to run with the ball as fast as they can around the post and back to the starting line. The faster team wins and receives a point for the round.

Game Description On command the first player of each team takes off, runs around the post and gives the ball to the next player behind the starting line, who takes off, and so on.

Crossing the starting line too early leads to disqualification.

A round is over when the last player of one team has crossed the starting line.

Variations 1. Shortening or lengthening the distance to run. 2. Passing the ball to the next player after running around the post.

Comments The distance to run must be adjusted to the abilities of the players. The game can also be played indoors.

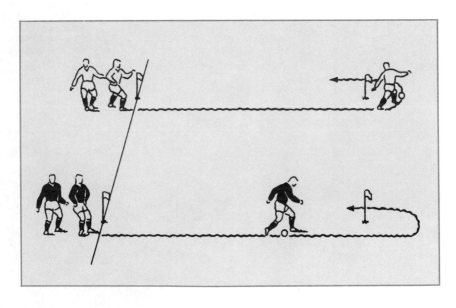

36 Hurdle Relay Game

Number of Players As many as desired, 2 equal teams.

Playing Field Starting line, several hurdles are on the 30 to 40 m-long running path.

Duration of Game Up to 20 min. or up to 10 heats for each team.

Objective of Game The players of both teams try to shoot the ball through each hurdle, to jump over the hurdle, and after going over the last, to run back beside the hurdles dribbling the ball. The faster team is the winner and receives a point for each round.

Game Description At the command, the first player of each team begins running. The next runs when the ball is given over to him behind the starting line. Stepping over the line too early leads to disqualification. A round is over when the last player of one team has crossed the starting line on his way back.

Variations 1. The ball is dribbled around the hurdles. 2. Run or crawl around the hurdles.

Comments Adjust the height of the hurdles and the distance to be run to the abilities of the players. The game can be played indoors.

Drills and Games for Agility

37   Game with a Rugby Ball

Purpose Teaching reaction ability.

Number of Players 2 teams with 5 to 11 players each.

Playing Field Half or entire soccer pitch, depending on the number of players.

Duration of Game Up to 45 min.

Objective of Game One team attacks to score goals, the other defends and tries to win the ball.

Game Description Two teams play according to the soccer rules, but setting is too loose without an offside. With smaller teams, the last player is goalkeeper and can handle the ball.

Variations 1. All the variations of small field soccer. 2. At the command of the trainer, change the goal that is to be attacked without interrupting the game.

Comments The particular effect of this game comes from the shape of the ball, which can change the flow of the game unpredictably. The danger of injury, especially in one-on-ones, increases in this game. The game leader must do his best to minimize this danger.

The game is suitable for advanced players.

38 Crab Soccer

Purpose Teaching skill and agility.

Number of Players 2 teams of 2 to 6 players.

Playing Field 20 x 10 m, with 2 small field goals on the touch lines.

Duration of Game Up to 20 min.

Objective of Game One team attacks and tries to score and, if the ball is lost, to prevent scoring on its own goal.

Game Description All players except for the goalkeepers must move and dribble the ball in a crab walk. Handling the ball is forbidden for the players on the field. Hands must always be on the ground. Breaking this rule is penalized by a free kick. The goalkeeper may kneel and may handle the ball. When the ball goes into touch or after foul play it is brought into play again with a free kick. Offside is lifted.

Variations Increase the stress by not allowing the buttocks to touch the ground at certain times.

Comments The number of players can be increased to 8 per team if the playing field is increased to 30 x 15 m. This game is especially suited for training indoors and also recommmended for advanced players.

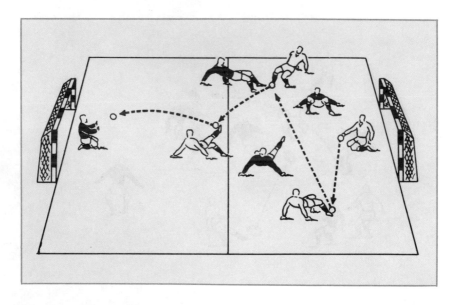

39   Bodiless Soccer

Purpose Teaching feel for the ball.

Number of Players 8 players, 4-on-4

Playing Field 40 x 25 m, 2 small field goals.

Duration of Game Up to 40 min.

Objective of Game Each team tries to score goals using high and half-high passing in the air. The opponent is not allowed to fight the team with the ball as is usual. It may only block the path of the player with ball.

Game Description One player starts the game by passing the ball to a teammate. The ball may not fall to the ground or be touched by one player more than three times in a row. If this happens, the ball is given to the opponent. The game is played without regular goalkeepers. Handling the ball is not allowed.

Comments Less experienced players can be touch the ball as often as they want. Technically good players should touch the ball no more than twice in a row. This game is especially suitable for very skilled players.

40   Game with Three Neutrals

Purpose Teaching feel for the ball

Number of Players 2 teams with 4 players each and 3 neutrals.

Playing Field 40 m x 25 m; 2 small field goals.

Duration of Game Up to 40 min.

Objective of Game Each team tries to score by using high or half-high passing in the air. The neutrals always play with the team that has the ball in order to ensure its numerical superiority.

Game Description One player begins the game by passing the ball to a teammate. The ball may not fall to the ground or be touched more than 3 times in a row by one player. The opponent gets the ball if this occurs or if he captures the ball. The game is played without regular goalkeepers. Handling the ball is not allowed.

Variations The number of times the ball may be touched can be changed.

Comments The smaller the team and the larger the number of neutrals, the easier the game will be (for example, 2 on 2 with five neutrals).

41   Parallel Four Goal Game

Purpose Training peripheral vision (space orientation).

Number of Players 2 teams with 6 to 11 players each.

Playing Field Soccer pitch with 2 goals on each long side; halfway line

Duration of Game Up to 60 min.

Objective of Game One team attacks in order to score on one of the two opposing goals. If it loses the ball, it defends its own goals.

Game Description A goal is scored when the ball rolls over the line of one of the two opponents' goals. The opponent gets the ball after goals, if he captures it, if the ball goes into touch, and after foul play. The game is played without offside, but with a corner ball. The kick-off on the halfway line is left out. After a goal, the game continues from the goal with a goal kick.

Variations 1. Play with two regular goalkeepers. 2. All players take part in the field play. The last player in front of his own goal may handle the ball.

Comments The farther away the goals on the touch lines are, the more successful the game movement is. The game is recommended for advanced players.

42 Three Goal Game

Purpose Training peripheral vision (space orientation).

Number of Players 2 teams with 8 players each, 1 neutral goalkeeper

Playing Field Half of the soccer pitch; 2 small field goals in addition to the standard goal on the side.

Duration of Game Up to 60 min.

Objective of Game One team attacks to score on one of the three goals. If the ball is lost, it defends the goals.

Game Description Goals can be scored in each of the three goals; the small field goals must be defended without help of the hands. If an attack has been checked by the defending team, one of the other goals must be attacked next, in order to prevent easy goals.

Variations 1. Specify the number of times the ball may be touched, or the period of time in which a goal must be scored. 2. On the command of the trainer, immediately change the goal being attacked.

Comments The corresponding target positions can be assigned before hand, one to each team, through rule limitations. The game is suitable for advanced players.

43   Game with Three Goals Next to Each Other

Purpose Training peripheral vision (space orientation).

Number of Players 2 teams with 4 to 6 players; 1 neutral goalkeeper

Playing Field Half of the soccer pitch; 3 makeshift goals, 1. 50 m wide and 5 m apart.

Duration of Game Up to 40 min.

Objective of Game Both teams try to kick the ball through one of the three makeshift goals to score. Only one goalkeeper is responsible for all three goals.

Game Description The game begins with a neutral goal kick by the goalkeeper. A team has scored a goal when the ball goes over the goal line inside the flag goal. A goal can be scored from both sides. Two goals, one after another, is not possible. The game is only interrupted for balls going into touch, with foul play and if the goalkeeper catches the ball. It is continued with a goal throw, free kick, or goal kick.

Variations The width of the goals and distance between them can be changed.

Comments The game is better with two goalkeepers, who can relieve each other. It is suitable for advanced players.

44   Game with Two Balls

Purpose Training peripheral vision (space orientation).

Number of Players 2 teams with 5 to 7 players each.

Playing Field Half of soccer pitch without goals.

Duration of Game Up to 30 min.

Objective of Game To score points, one team must have both balls for a certain amount of time. In case of loss of the ball, interfere with the opponent and prevent teamwork.

Game Description One team has both balls and begins the game. It receives one point if it holds on to both balls for two minutes. The game continues until the opponent has captured a ball. The opposing team then gets both balls and the game begins again.

Variations 1. Adjust the length of time the ball must be held (between 1 and 5 minutes) according to the abilities of the players. 2. Rate the score according to game errors, not according to time. After each error, the opponent gets both balls. 3. Teams with a greater number of players must use the whole soccer pitch. It is useful to have two referees, one to follow each ball.

Comment The game is suitable for advanced players.

Drills and Games for Teaching Technique

Receiving and Passing the Ball

Soccer Tennis

45   Soccer Tennis (Singles)

Number of Players 2 players, one on one.

Playing Field 12 x 16, divided into two fields on the halfway line by a 1 m high net.

Duration of Game 2 winning sets up to 21 points.

Objective of Game To score a point, both players must hit the ball over the net into the opponents' half and may not touch it more than once. The player who scores 21 points is the set winner. The winner is the player who has won two sets. In tie-breakers in the third set, sides are changed after 10 points.

Game Description The game begins in the opposing half with the serve. The ball may bounce once in the opponent's field before being played back. Direct play with the head or foot is allowed. Each player has five serves in a row. The serve follows an error. An error is committed when the ball touches the net during the serve, lands outside the field, bounces more than once, or is hit with the hand.

Variations Demand various forms of kicking for the serve.

Comments Adjust playing field size to the skill of the players. The game can be played indoors.

46   Soccer Tennis (Doubles)

Number of Players 4 players, 2-on-2.

Playing Field 16 x 8 m, divided into 2 fields by a 1 m high net; a line marked lengthways divides each field in half once more.

Duration of Game See game 45.

Objective of Game See game 45.

Game Description See game 45. In addition, the following conditions should be noted: 1. The serve always comes from the right half of one's own playing half, and the left half of one's opponents'. Only afterwards can the game be played from both halves. 2. The ball is always kicked alternately. The player who has just kicked the ball over the net must leave the next ball to his partner. Playing the ball twice in a row counts as an error and a point for the opponent. 3. After every change of serve, the partners change places.

Variations See game 45.

Comments The game can be played indoors.

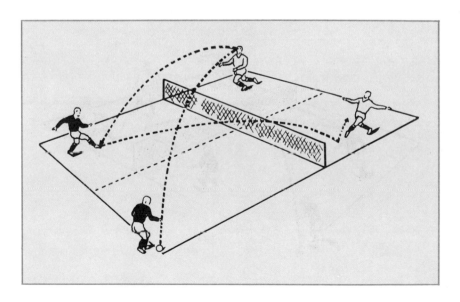

47　Soccer Tennis (Team)

Number of Players 2 teams with 3 or 4 players each.

Playing Field Approximately 10 x 20.

Duration of Game See game 45.

Objective of Game See game 45.

Game Description See game 45. The following exceptions have been
added: 1. The players of each team receive the numbers 1 to
3, or 1 to 4; 2. The ball can be hit three or four times within the
team, depending upon previous agreement. In doing this, it is
possible that a player hits the ball twice if another has hit it in
between. Touching the ball two or more times in a row is not
allowed in this game.

Variations See game 45.

Comments The game can be played indoors.

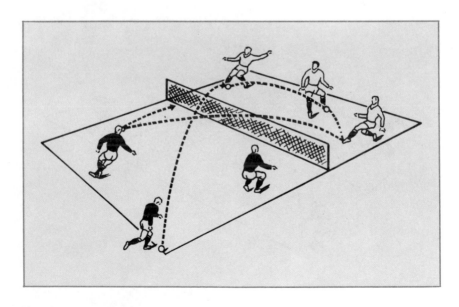

48 Soccer Tennis with a Prohibited Zone

Number of Players 2 teams with 2 player each.

Playing Field 22 x 8 m, divided into 2 fields by a 1 m high net; 3 m wide prohibited zones are marked in front of, behind, and parallel to the net.

Duration of Game See game 45.

Objective of Game See game 45.

Game Description See game 45 and the following special rules: 1. To score a point the ball must go over the net and the prohibited zones. Higher demands are made on the technique of the players since the ball has a longer way to cover. If the ball goes into the prohibited zone, it counts as a mistake, and a point for the opponent. 2. Touching the ball two or more times in a row is allowed in this game. The ball may also be passed between players as long as desired. The important thing is that here, too, the ball may only bounce once.

Variations See game 45.

Comments The size of the prohibited area should be adjusted to the abilities of the players. The game can be played indoors.

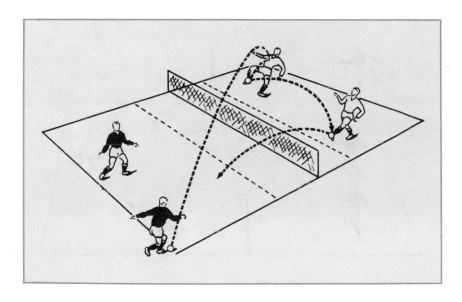

49   Soccer Tennis through Two Ropes

Number of Players 2 teams of three players each.

Playing Field 18 x 9 m, divided into 2 fields by 2 ropes; one rope at a height of 1 m, the other at 3 m.

Duration of Game See game 45.

Objective of Game See game 45.

Game Description Each team serves alternatively 5 times. The serve follows each mistake behind one's own boundary. An error is committed when the ball:
1. does not go between the two ropes:
2. lands outside of the field;
3. bounces more than once; or
4. is hit with the hand.

If the ball touches the rope, the game continues as long as it does not change sides above or below.

Variations See game 45.

Comments The better the ability of the players, the smaller the distance between the ropes. The game can be played indoors.

Kicking with the Inside of the Foot

50   Two Field Game

Number of Players 2 teams with 8 players each.

Playing Field Soccer pitch divided into 2 fields by a 20 m wide zone, 10 m left and right of the halfway line.

Duration of Game Up to 40 min.

Objective of Game Four attackers play against four fullbacks in each half of the field. The attackers try to score goals, while the fullbacks try to prevent a success. The middle section may be bridged by long kicks.

Game Description If a fullback captures the ball, he passes the ball to his partners in the other game half. The middle section may not be crossed by any player. The midfield may be bridged by long passes. Offside is lifted.

Variations 1. With first-time passing, the fullback must get the ball out of his half with three passes. 2. The number of players may be increased to 12.

Comments Depending on the target position, it is possible to allow advantages through regulations to both groups.

51 Six Goal Game

Number of Players 2 teams with 5 players each.

Playing Field Half of the soccer pitch; 6 makeshift goals (flagstaffs), 1 m wide.

Duration of Game Up to 60 minutes.

Objective of Game Both teams try to kick a ball through a goal and score, and if the ball is lost, to prevent scoring.

Game Description A goal counts when the ball goes over the goal line between the flagstaffs and reaches one's own team-mate. If if flies over the staffs, a goal is not recognized. Goals can be scored from both sided of the goal. After a goal is scored, the game continues on the other side without interruption. Two goals in a row on the same goal is not possible.

VariationsThe playing leg for the goal shot is designated.

Comments The number and width of the goal is to be adjusted to the abilities of the players. Teams with more than five players practise on two fields. Only teams with an equal number of players should play against each other. The game is suitable for advanced players.

52   Monkey in the Middle

Number of Players 3 players.

Playing Field 24 x 8 m, divided by 3 lines into 3 equal fields.

Duration of Game Up to 30 min.

Objective of Game Both outer players kick the ball over the field of the middle player so that, if possible, he will not reach the ball. The middle player tries to catch the ball. The winner is the player with the least minus points.

Game Description In each field is a player. The two outer players hit the ball to each other directly as a fly ball. The middle player tries to stop the ball using soccer techniques. The fly balls may only bounce once. A player gets a minus point if the ball bounces more than once in his field, if the ball does not hit the field of his partner, or if the ball is stopped by the middle player. The middle player is changed at regular intervals.

Variations Designate the playing leg and possibly allow touching the ball twice.

Comments The game can be played indoors.

53   Target Ball through the Goals

Number of Players 2 teams with as many players as desired.

Playing Field Chalk out several 20 x 6 m fields; mark a 1.50 m wide goal in the middle of the field with flagstaffs.

Duration of Game Up to 30 min.

Objective of Game All players try to kick the ball through their goal to score. The winner is the one who has scored the most goals after a certain time.

Game Description A goal has been scored if the ball is kicked from behind the boundary and rolls through between the two flag-staffs. If the ball flies over the staffs, the opponent receives the ball, and the goal is not valid. Balls hit directly back through the goal are worth two goals. After half time, the sides are exchanged. Each team must count its goals itself. Only at the end is the winner declared.

Variations 1. Designate the playing leg. 2. Lengthen the playing field to 40 m.

Comments A goal can be set up at the end of the playing field to prevent spin kicks. The game can be played indoors.

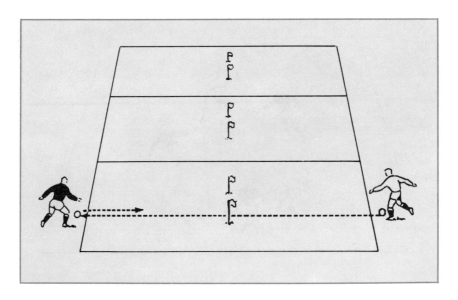

54   Circle Ball Game

Number of Players 2 teams with 3 players each.

Playing Field Half of the soccer pitch, in the middle of which is a circle with a radius of 8 m, with a medicine ball as a target in the middle of the circle.

Duration of Game Up to 30 min.

Objective of Game The team with the ball tries to accumulate points by hitting the ball in the middle of the circle.

Game Description The circle may not be entered. If the ball goes into touch or remains lying in the circle, the game is continued with a throw-in. After each hit, the medicine ball is moved back to the middle.

Variations 1. The number of players is changed; with uneven numbers, the game is played with a neutral, making the attackers the majority. 2. A rugby ball may be used to add some fun to the game. 3. Double Circle Game: 2 teams with 4 players each. Each team has a circle.

Comments This game is also suitable for smaller indoor facilities in which walls can be used as passing barriers.

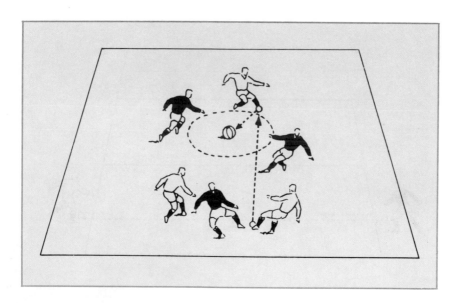

55   Soccer Target Kick Game

Number of Players 2 teams with 3 to 4 players.

Playing Field 40 X 20 m, with a 3 m wide zone on both sides in which 3 clubs each are set up at equal distances.

Duration of Game Up to 30 min.

Objective of Game Both teams try to hit or knock down the opponent's clubs, and try to prevent shots on their own clubs.

Game Description A team begins the game in its own half. It attacks the club zone of the opponents and tries to knock over as many clubs as possible. If the opponent captures the ball, the game changes over to them. The same applies to hits and balls going into touch. The club zone may not be entered.

Variations Specify whether the target kick may be made with both legs, or with one or the other.

Comments The game is especially suited for a gymnasium. Balls rebounding from the wall and knocking over clubs are not counted as hits.

56   Four Field Alley Game

Number of Players 16 players, 8-on-8.

Playing Field 40 x 20 m; 3 lines marking 4 equal fields.

Duration of Game Up to 20 min.

Objective of Game Both teams are divided into groups of four players. The fields are occupied so that each group is between opposing groups. To win points, the ball must kicked through between the row of opponents to their own team opposite them.

Game Description One team begins the game. It may keep the ball until there is a favourable opportunity to pass in the alley. The opponent gets the ball if it stops the ball or if the ball goes into touch. Handling the ball and stepping out of your own field is not allowed. The game may be played to head height.

Variations 1. Limit the number of passes within a group. 2. Designate the playing leg and the number of times the ball may be touched. 3. Play with two balls.

Comment In a game with two balls, two referees are necessary.

57　Alley Game

Number of Players　2, 4, or 8 players.

Playing Field　Central circle, with flagstaffs positioned randomly inside the circle.

Duration of Game　Up to 20 min.

Objective of Game　Two players of each team standing across each other run around the circle with the ball and try to pass it through an alley to accumulate points. A point is given for every successful pass.

Game Description　Entering the circle to pass the ball is not allowed. After each pass, the active players must run farther to change their positions. Passes on the edge of the circle are not valid; the ball must pass at least two flagstaffs.

Variations　1. The number of flagstaffs is increased or decreased. 2. The radius of the circle is changed. 3. The flagstaffs are continually moved.

Comments　This game is suitable for players of all ages and abilities and can be played indoors.

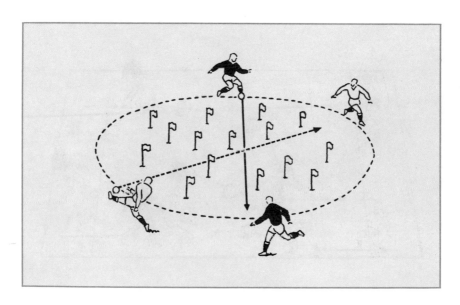

58   Push Ball

Purpose Teaching scoring accuracy.

Number of Players 2 teams with 3 to 4 players.

Playing Field Gymnasium with 2 clearly marked goal lines.

Duration of Game Up to 2 x 2 min.

Objective of Game Each team tries to score by pushing the medicine ball assigned to it over the opponents' line by means of well-aimed shots. The medicine balls are marked differently for identification.

Game Description Each team gets a soccer ball and, on the whistle, begins the game behind its own line. Each team can kick its own ball to push the medicine ball over the opponent's line and score, or fight the opponents' attack to prevent the opponents from scoring. The game is over when all three medicine balls cross the opponents' line.

Variations Specify various methods of kicking, and designate the playing leg.

Comments This game is especially suitable for indoor soccer.

Shooting on Goal with the Instep

59 Shooting Semi-Circle (Half of the Penalty Area)

Number of Players 2 teams with 4 players each and 1 neutral goalkeeper.

Playing Field Half the soccer pitch with 1 standard goal and shooting circle (penalty area).

Duration of Game Up to 60 min.

Objective of Game A team attacks and may score only from outside the shooting circle. If possession of the ball is lost, the team tries to prevent the opponents from scoring.

Game Description The game begins with a neutral goal kick by the goalkeeper. The shooting circle may be entered and passed from for a goal shot. The game is played without offside or corner balls. Balls going into touch, go the goalkeeper. If they are outside the shooting circle, the game continues with a throw-in.

Variations Designate the playing leg for the goal shot and specify other methods of kicking.

Comments The distance of the shooting circle from the goal should be adjusted according to the abilities of the players. For less experienced players the shooting circle should be at least 8 m; for more experienced players it should be 18 m large at the most. The game is suitable for advanced players.

60　Forced to Shoot

Number of Players　2 teams with 2 to 5 players and one neutral goalkeeper.

Playing Field　Half of the soccer pitch with standard goal.

Duration of Game　Up to 60 min.

Objective of Game　One team attacks and tries to score goals, and if the ball is lost, to prevent scoring.

Game Description　The goalkeeper begins the game with a neutral goal kick. The player who is the second on his team to receive a pass, is forced to make a goal shot. The opponent gets the ball if he captures it, if the ball goes into touch, and after an error (if a player other than the second shoots for the goal), as well as after foul play. The goalkeeper brings the ball back into the game with a neutral goal kick if he catches the ball, if the ball goes into touch over the extended goal line, and after a goal is scored.

Variations　The playing leg for the goal shot and the method of kicking are specified.

Comments　In games with two-on-two the first player to touch the ball is forced to shoot. In games with 4 players on a team, the third player is forced to shoot.

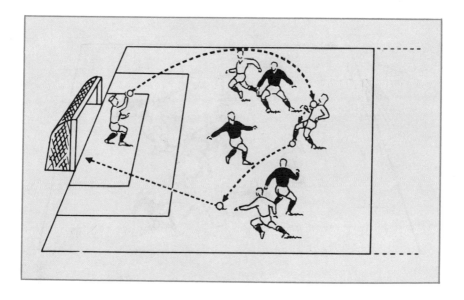

61   Game with an Open Goal

Number of Players   2 teams with 4 players each and 1 neutral
    goalkeeper.

Playing Field As large as desired, with a 6 to 7 m wide goal in the middle.

Duration of Game   Up to 30 min.

Objective of Game One team attacks and tries to score goals and, if the
    ball is lost, to prevent scoring.

Game Description   A goal can be scored from both sides of the
    flagstaffs. If the ball goes through the goal, the game is
    continued on the other side without interruption. If the ball flies
    over the flags (no goal) the game is continued as well. Balls
    caught by the goalkeeper are brought back into play by a neutral
    goal kick. Balls going into touch are thrown in.

Variations 1. Designate the playing leg for the goal shot and specify the
    method of kicking. 2. Increase the number of players to six-on-
    six.

Comments The game may be played with two goalkeepers, who may
    relieve each other in order to alleviate the pressure.

62   Shooting on Goal Game

Number of Players   2 teams with 4 to 5 players each.

Playing Field   Double penalty area with 2 standard goals; penalty area line serves as halfway line.

Duration of Game   Up to 30 min.

Objective of Game   Each team must shoot the ball from its own half into the opponents' goal. The team with the ball looks for favourable shooting positions, while the opponent tries to block the shots.

Game Description   The goalkeeper begins the game with a goal throw to a teammate. The ball may be shot immediately from a favourable position, otherwise the ball may remain with the team for three first-time passes. The halfway line may not be crossed. Balls going into touch are brought back into the game by a throw-in or kick-in.

Variations   1. Changing the method of kicking; inner or outer instep kicking. 2. The playing leg is designated.

Comments   In order to improve shooting accuracy, the game may be played with a small field goal. In this case, handling the ball is not permitted.

63   Shooting Game with a Rebound Wall

Number of Players 2 teams with 4 players each.

Playing Field 30 x 20 m, 2 small field goals stand 6 m in front of 2 rebound walls limiting the playing field, with the goal opening towards them. Indoors the gymnasium wall can serve as a rebound wall.

Duration of Game Up to 50 min.

Objective of Game Each team tries — preferrably through indirect playing against the rebound wall — to score goals and prevent scoring by the opponent.

Game Description Both teams play into the backwards goals. A goal is scored when the ball has gone over the goal line. The aim, however, is to score a goal with a strong shot on the rebound wall; this counts double, or even more. Handling the ball and foul play are penalized by a free kick against the wall that may not be defended. A goal scored in this way counts as a single goal.

Variations On command of the coach, if the ball is in midfield, the other goal is attacked.

Comments If scoring using the rebound wall is infrequent, the defense possibilities may be restricted by a goal circle that may not be entered. The game is suitable for advanced players.

64 Free Kick Game

Number of Players 2 teams with 3 to 5 players each, 1 neutral goalkeeper.

Playing Field Approximately 70 x 30 m, or width of soccer pitch x 30 m. A standard goal is set up 30 m opposite a small field goal.

Duration of Game Up to 30 min.

Objective of Game Two teams play against each other. They alternate kicking the ball from the boundary of the penalty area to the standard goal guarded by the goalkeeper. Any player who scores a goal may shoot again. If the goalkeeper stops the ball, he throws it to the opposing team which, by attacking the goal, can score another point.

Game Description If the attack on the goal fails or if the ball goes into touch, then this team keeps the ball and continues free kicking. Handling the ball in front of the small field goal is not allowed. All players must take part in the free kicking in a certain order.

Variations 1. Designate the playing leg and specify other methods of kicking (outer and inner instep). 2. Play this game as a penalty kick game.

65   Shooting Wall Game

Number of Players 2 teams with 2 players each.

Playing Field Shooting wall, with a prohibited zone 4 m wide in front of it, followed by a playing field 10 m long.

Duration of Game 2 winning sets up to 15 points.

Objective of Game Collect bonus points on the target area kicking with the instep.

Game Description The game begins with a serve from the playing field. The serve changes to the opponent after every error. An error occurs whenever the ball: 1. bounces in the prohibited area; 2. does not bounce over the line against the wall; 3. bounces more than once in the playing field; 4. is hit by the same player twice. Errors are bonus points for the opponent.

Variation Specify the method of kicking for the serve.

Comments The dimensions for the prohibited zone and the playing field must be adjusted according to the abilities of the players. Beginners can play without a prohibited zone. The game can be played in a gymnasium and is suitable for advanced players.

66   Push the Ball

Number of Players   2 teams with 3 to 7 players each.

Playing Field 40 x 20 m; lines 10 m apart mark 4 fields; a medicine ball is on the halfway line.

Duration of Game   Up to 25 min.

Objective of Game   Each team tries, through aimed strong shots, to hit the medicine ball lying in the middle and to push it onto the opponents' side. If the medicine ball is hit, the team receives one point. If the team succeeds in pushing the medicine ball over the 10 m line, the team gets three points.

Game Description   The players, each with a ball, stand on their respective starting lines. The medicine ball is on the halfway line. On command, they try to hit the medicine ball. Any ball that crosses into the opponent's field may be used by the opponents.

Variations   Specify other methods of kicking for the target kick. Pay attention to practising with both legs.

Comments   In this game it is useful for each team to have a referee. The game may also be played indoors.

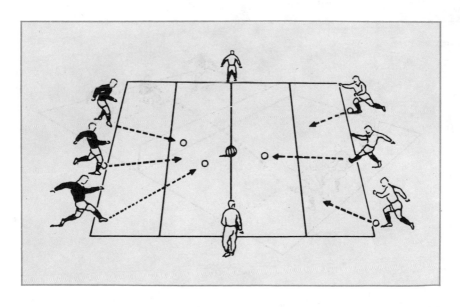

67   Ball under the Rope

Number of Players 2 teams with 3 to 5 players each.

Playing Field 30 m x 15 m with 2 areas 5 m wide on the sides and a rope stretched 1 m high over the halfway line.

Duration of Game Up to 20 min.

Objective of Game Each team occupies a 5 m area. Both teams can score a goal if they kick the ball under the rope and over the opponents' back line.

Game Description The 5 m area may not be crossed during the kick. Kicks against or over the rope are invalid. The player who has caught the ball must kick. Balls bouncing back belong to the players who receive them first. The ball may be caught with the hands.

Variations 1. Play with 2 or 3 balls. 2. Allow only first-time passes or kick with a certain foot. 3. Change the height of the rope.

Comments Adjust width of the playing field in accordance with the number and abilities of the players. This game is especially suitable for a gymnasium of the specified dimensions.

Kicking with the Instep

68   Game with Blocked-off Midfield

Number of Players 2 teams with 5 players each.

Playing Field 40 m x 20 m, 2 small field goals with openings outward.

Duration of Game Up to 40 min.

Objective of Game The team with the ball attacks the goal of its opponent. A goal can be scored only if the ball has been passed over the blocked-off midfield.

Game Description A team begins the game from its own goal. The ball must be passed over the midfield before shooting on the goal is allowed. If the ball touches the midfield, the opponent may throw the ball in from the spot where the ball has crossed the line. These players may run over the midfield. The last player of the defending team may handle the ball.

Variations 1. Increase the width of the playing field and number the players to 7-on-7. Handling the ball is not allowed. 2. Cross the midfield by playing the ball in the air. If the ball touches the ground, the opponent receives a free kick from where it lands.

Comments The game is recommended for advanced players.

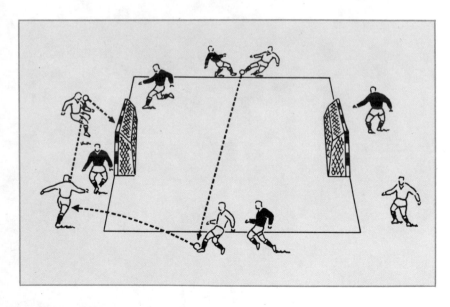

69 Circle Targets

Number of Players As many as desired; several teams; 1-on-1.

Playing Field 40 m x 20 m, 3 circles in each half; 1 circle 10 m, and 2 circles 15 m from the halfway line. The radius of the circles is approximately 3 m.

Duration of Game Up to 20 min. or up to 20 hits.

Objective of Game Each player stands within a circle in his half and tries to kick the ball into a circle in the other half. If he succeeds, he has scored and is awarded a point.

Game Description Only high balls count as hits. A point is taken away for balls not reaching the halfway line or going over the boundary. The ball may not be kicked twice in a row from the same circle.

Variations 1. The opponent can prevent scoring by blocking the ball before it hits the circle. Hitting with the hand is not allowed. 2. Hits from balls kicked back directly count for two points.

Comments Mark the circles clearly (possibly with flags etc.).

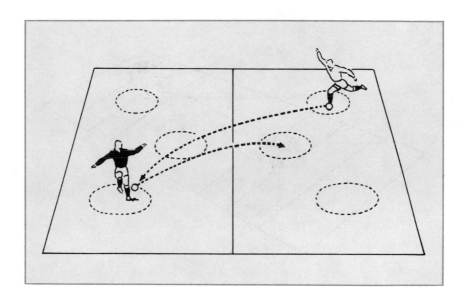

70 High Ball Game

Number of Players As many as desired, several teams, 1-on-1.

Playing Field 40 m x 10 m, 3 zones on each side, the outer zone is 4 m wide, the 2 others, 3 m wide.

Duration of Game Up to 30 min.

Objective of Game Each player tries to kick the ball from one zone in his half to the same zone in the opponent's half to score. Hits can be valued differently; for balls from:
zone I to zone I (20 to 26 m) = 1 point,
zone II to zone II (26 to 32 m) = 2 points,
zone III to zone III (32 to 40 m) = 3 points.

Game Description Only high balls that have not first touched the ground are valid. After a certain time, all the results are tallied and the winning team is declared.

Variations 1. Hits from directly kicked balls count double. 2. At least ten kicks must be made from every zone.

Comments Pay attention to practising with both feet. Also, mark the zones clearly (possibly also with flags on the sideline).

71   Tower Ball Game

Number of Players 2 teams with as many players as desired.

Playing Field 40 m x 15 m, in the middle of the field are 2 gymnastic boxes on which lie several medicine balls.

Duration of Game Up to 40 min.

Objective of Game Both teams try to score by shooting at the medicine balls from behind their touch lines. A point is given for each hit.

Game Description Valid hits are only those shots that hit the medicine balls. Balls that fall from the boxes because they were jarred do not count. Any player who hits the box must replace the fallen balls himself. The opponent accomplishes this with genuine hits. Stepping over the front line is not allowed.

Variations 1. Practise with both feet. 2. Include other methods of kicking. 3. Increase distance from the middle to the touch line to 30 m.

Comments Two referees are useful, each observing one team. The game may be played indoors if the size of the playing area is reduced.

72   High Ball Relay Game

Number of Players 2 teams with as many players as desired.

Playing Field Soccer field; two longitudinal lines from penalty area to penalty area, 4 playing field corners.

Duration of Game Up to 10 starts per player.

Objective of Game Each player of a team can score a point, if he runs to the center line with the ball and passes to his teammate in the corner of the field with an instep kick.

Game Description Both teams take positions diagonally behind the playing corners. Each team has a ball. On command, the first player of each team runs to the halfway line with the ball. From there, they hit it sideways into their team's corners, run after it at an angle over the field, and take position behind the group. The game is over when every player is back in his starting position. Only high balls that land in the corners of the playing field are valid.

Variations 1. The winner is the team that has finished a round first.
2. Change corners after each round.

Comments Well-suited for advanced teams.

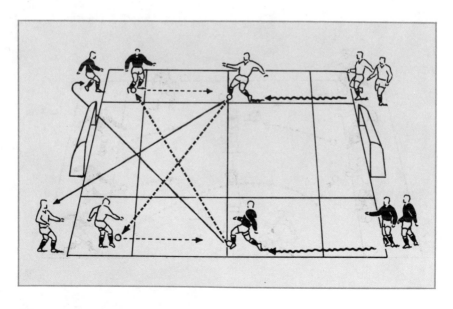

Dribbling

73 Open Goal in a Circle

Number of Players As many as desired, in groups of 2.

Playing Field 20 m x 20 m, in the middle is a 2 m wide goal marked by flags.

Duration of Game Up to 5 x 2 min.

Objective of Game A player tries to dribble around his opponent to score.

Game Description After a goal is scored, the other player gets the ball. If the opponent wins the ball, or the ball crosses the touch line, the opposing player becomes the attacker. Easy goals are not allowed. For this reason, the ball must be out of the circle before the goal may be attacked again.

Variations 1. The 5 m circle may not be entered. The marking serves as a shooting circle. 2. Specify various methods of dribbling.

Comments In setting up breaks, it is useful to choose simple technical exercises. The game is suitable for advanced players.

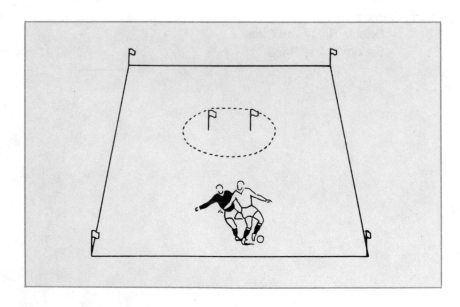

74   Stage Game

Number of Players 2 teams with 6 to 8 players each.

Playing Field Soccer field with 4 equal fields.

Duration of Game Up to 60 min.

Objective of Game One team attacks, the other defends. The attacker must cover each of the opponents' stages by dribbling over the line. A goal is scored only when the shot comes from the stage in front of the opponents' goal. The opponent gets the ball if he wins it, if the ball goes out of play, and if the stage mark is passed over instead of dribbled over. Then the game changes to the other side. The game is played with regular goalkeepers but without offside. The goalkeepers may support the attacks of their teams.

Variations Demand various forms of dribbling.

Comments This game is especially suitable for players who have mastered the basic skills of dribbling.

75 Shooting Circle Dribbling

Number of Players 2 teams with 6 players each.

Playing Field Sideways across half a soccer field; 2 small field goals with a shooting circle of 12m to 20 m.

Duration of Game Up to 40 min.

Objective of Game A team tries to penetrate the opponents' shooting circle by dribbling and to score a goal. The opponents defend their goal.

Game Description One team attacks. It can only score goals if a player succeeds in breaking into the shooting circle by dribbling. Scoring through skillful teamwork may also be attempted in the shooting circle. Shots taken from outside the circle are invalid and are penalized by a free kick.

Variations 1. Vary the method of dribbling. 2. Change the number of players and the playing field size. 3. Play with all the variations of small field soccer (for example; low, only left, etc.).

Comments The greater the abilities and technical expertise of the players, the smaller the shooting circle should be, and vice versa. The game is suitable for advanced players.

76 Ball over the Line

Number of Players 10 to 12 players, 5-on-5, or 6-on-6.

Playing Field Sideways across a soccer field.

Duration of Game Up to 30 min.

Objective of Game Each team tries to keep one player free so that he can dribble the ball over the goal line and score a goal.

Game Description The game is played without goalkeepers and offsides. If a team loses the ball to the opponent, the game changes to the other side. The goal line is the entire sideline. After each goal the opponent gets the ball. The winner is the team to score the most goals after a certain time.

Variations 1. Designate the foot the ball must be dribbled with. 2. Specify the method of dribbling (for example, with the inside of the foot, with the instep, etc.).

Comments This game is suitable for advanced players.

77   Lane Game

Number of Players 2 teams with 4 to 6 players each.

Playing Field Soccer field marked with longitudinal lanes of equal lengths; the number of lanes is one more than the number of players on each team (for example, for 4 players 5 lanes, for 6 players 7 lanes).

Duration of Game Up to 40 min.

Objective of Game One team attacks to score goals, the other defends. If a player gets the ball in a free lane, he may run with the ball without being attacked.

Game Description When changing lanes, the ball must be dribbled over the line, and the opponent may attack again. Passing over free lanes is not allowed. A shot is only allowed after a lane change. The game is played without regular goalkeepers. The last player of each team may handle the ball. Balls going out of play and corner kicks are dribbled back in. Offside is removed.

Variations Specify the method of dribbling and the playing foot.

Comments Adjust size of the playing field to the abilities of the players.

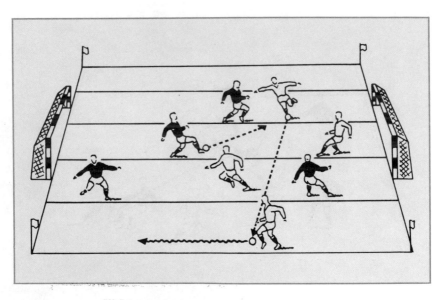

78   Bridge Guards

Number of Players 2 teams with 6 players each.

Playing Field 60 m x 20 m, 6 equal fields.

Duration of Game Up to 10 dribblings for each team.

Objective of Game One team attacks, the other defends. Each player of the attacking team has a ball. A point is scored only if the dribbler succeeds in getting his ball through the blocked zone and crossing the target line. The defenders occupy every 2 fields as a blocked zone and are divided into 3 groups of 3 players, 2 players, and 1 player. They try to take the ball away from the attacking players.

Game Description On command, the attackers begin. Any player who loses his ball or is crowded over the sideline, drops out until the next round. The defenders may not leave the blocked zone. The attacking players may gather in the zones between for a renewed attack. After every round, the teams change roles. The winner is declared at the end of all the rounds.

Comments Call on the fairness of the players to prevent injuries in 1-on-1 situations. By reducing the size of the playing field, the game can be played indoors.

99

79　Dribbling Tag

Number of Players　2 teams of 4 to 8 players each.

Playing Field　Penalty area divided by a line.

Duration of Game　Up to 20 min.

Objective of Game　Each team occupies one field. Each team sends a player to the opponent with the assignment to tag as many players as possible without losing the ball himself.

Game Description　A point is given for every tagged player, when a player loses the ball, or when he dribbles it over the boundary. If the catcher loses the ball, he drops out and another player on his team takes over his task. The result is declared after all players have been catchers. Two referees are necessary for this game, each of whom must monitor the player in the opposing half, and count the players he tags.

Variations　1. A time limit for the catchers of 2 to 4 minutes. 2. Specify the method of dribbling and the playing leg.

Comments　The game can be played indoors.

80   Dribble Relay in a Circle

Number of Players As many as desired, 2 equal teams.

Playing Field Central circle with halfway line.

Duration of Game Up to 20 min. or 10 laps per team.

Objective of Game The players must dribble around the circle. Each player dribbles around the circle and passes the ball to the next player. The team that is back in position first, wins a point.

Game Description On command, the first player of each team begins his run on the opposite cross points of the halfway line and passes the ball from this point. When all players have run, the round is finished. Stepping inside the circle with the ball results in disqualification.

Variations 1. Vary the methods of dribbling. 2. Each player has a ball and all players attempt to execute the exercise simultaneously. 3. Specify several rounds, one after each other.

Comments Adjust the game to the abilities of the players. The game can be played indoors.

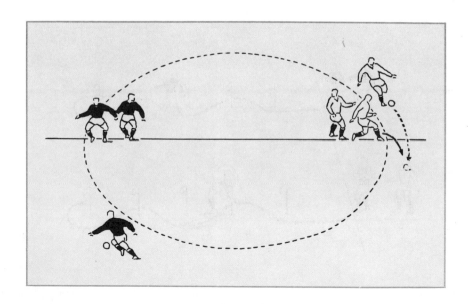

81   Slalom Relay Game

Number of Players As many as desired, 2 equal teams.

Playing Field Starting line, and 2 rows of flags 2 m apart.

Duration of Game Up to 20 min. or 10 heats per team.

Objective of Game The player of one team must run a slalom course marked by flags with the ball.

Game Description On command, the first player of each team begins his run. The next takes his turn after the ball is given to him behind the starting line. Stepping over the line too early leads to disqualification. A round is completed when all players have run. The faster team gets a point.

Variations 1. Vary the method of dribbling. 2. The dribbling will be made more difficult if the course is asymmetrical.

Comments This game is suitable for all age and performance groups and can also be played indoors.

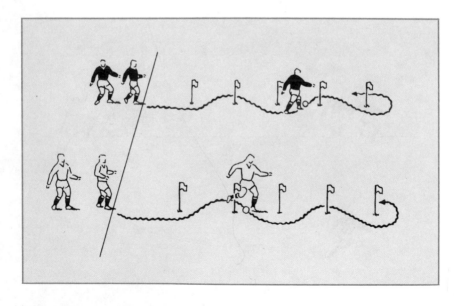

Heading

82 Heading for Goal

Number of Players 2 players, 1-on-1.

Playing Field 10 m x 5 up to 16 m x 8 m, chalk in the halfway line, mark goals on the corners with flags.

Duration of Game Up to 20 min. or to 10 goals with side change.

Objective of Game Both players try to head the ball over the opponents' goal and score. The winner is the player who has scored the most goals within a given period of time.

Game Description Game starts by throwing the ball up high. The player with the ball can hit it several times by juggling to the halfway line and may head it from there. The halfway line may not be crossed. Direct heading is allowed. If a player loses the ball by juggling, his opponent gets a free kick from the halfway line.

Variations 1. Without a halfway line. The ball can be juggled as far as desired and can be hit away by the opponent with his hand everywhere. 2. Several teams play at the same time in tournament form and declare the best. 3. Heading for goal in pairs. The ball may be headed back and forth as often as desired. If a pair loses the ball during the passing, the opponent gets a free kick from the center line.

Comments This game is suitable for players of all ages and abilities.

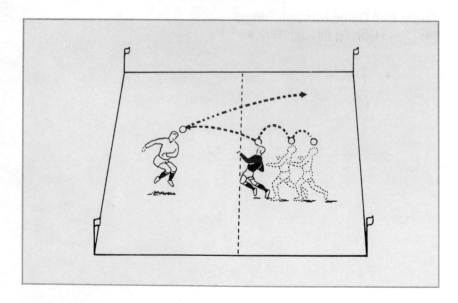

83   Heading Game from Midfield

Number of Players 8 players, 4-on-4, 2 each in midfield, and 1 in front of each goal as attacking and defending player.

Playing Field 30 m x 15 m; 2 small field goals opening outward; halfway line.

Duration of Game By intervals, 5 min, constantly alternating up to 6 x 5 min.

Objective of Game Scoring is attempted by accurate throws from midfield to the free running players in front of the goal and by heading the ball into the goal. When the ball is lost, it is fought for in the midfield with man-to-man marking.

Game Description A goal can only be scored with a throw from the opponents' half. In midfield, the ball is played with the hand only, and in front of the goal, with the head only. If the ball is lost, the opponent gets it.

Comments The set up with the hand is important for a header. While less experienced players may allow the ball to bounce as often as desired, bouncing is limited to direct play with experienced players. Adjust the duration and number of repetitions to the abilities of the players. The game is suitable for advanced players and can also be played indoors.

84 Heading Game with Four Neutrals

Number of Players 8 players — 2-on-2 and 4 neutrals.

Playing Field 40 m x 20 m, 2 small field goals.

Duration of Game Up to 40 min.

Objective of Game Two players defend their goal. The two others attack to score goals. The four neutrals always play with the attacking team.

Game Description One player begins and heads the ball to his teammate or to one of the four neutrals. The ball may only be played with the head. The ball may be touched as often as desired. The other side gains the advantage if the ball falls to the ground, or is captured by one of the two defenders. If the ball goes over the playing field boundary, the game is continued from there with a header.

Variations Limit the number of times the ball may be touched.

Comments This game is especially suited for players who have mastered the basics of heading technique. More experienced players require fewer neutrals; less experienced players, more neutrals. With the corresponding reduction in the number of neutrals, the game is suitable for advanced players. (With a smaller playing field, it may also be played indoors.)

85 Handball-Heading Game without a Throwing Circle

Number of Players 2 teams with 4 to 7 players each.

Playing Field 40 m x 20 m, 2 small field goals.

Duration of Game Up to 40 min.

Objective of Game One team begins the game by throwing the ball. A goal may be scored only by a header after a throw. The player with the ball is not allowed to throw up the ball so that he himself can head it. If the ball is lost, the opponent gets the ball, and the game changes to the other side. If the ball goes over one of the marked lines, there is a throw-in. The game is played without offsides and without regular goalkeepers. Any player may defend the goal and use his hands to catch the ball.

Variations 1. To head the ball into the goal more easily, use a larger goal. 2. Draw a defense line 10 m in front of the goal, behind which no team may have more than three players.

Comments The game is suitable, with corresponding stress, for players of all ages and abilities and can be played indoors.

86   High Heading Game

Number of Players 2 teams with 5 to 7 players each.

Playing Field 40 m x 20 m, 2 small field goals.

Duration of Game Up to 40 min.

Objective of Game One team defends the goal. The other attacks until it has scored a goal or lost the ball to the defending team. The winner is the team that scores the most goals in a given period of time.

Game Description Start the game by throwing the ball high in the air. The game may be played with the head only . Catching the ball in the air is not allowed. Only when the ball has touched the ground does the player who picks it up get to continue playing. A free header is awarded if rules are broken or if the ball crosses a marked line.

Variations Stipulate whether the player with the ball may score a goal himself or whether a goal may be scored only following a pass.

Comments Three players against three, or four against four, and a smaller playing field of 25 m x 20 m is possible for advanced teams. With these alternative specifications, the game can be played indoors.

87 Heading Tennis

Number of Players 2 teams with 6 to 8 players each.

Playing Field 18 m x 9 m (volleyball court), a net or a rope strung 1.5 m above the halfway line.

Duration of Game 2 winning sets up to 20 points. If each team wins a set, a tie-breaker takes place, at which point the sides are changed after 10 points.

Objective of Game The ball must be headed over the net into the opposing half and may only bounce once. Only the side which has the serve can win a point.

Game Description A player begins behind his own half and heads the ball to the opponent. With the serve, the opponent must let the ball bounce once before he plays it back. Otherwise, the ball can be headed directly back. Passing within a team is unlimited. A serve follows each mistake and must be made by a different player each time. The serve, if possible, should be made with the head. However, especially with a long game, it is possible to change these requirements so that the ball may be hit from the air with the knee or foot. An error occurs whenever:

1. the opponent does not let the ball bounce after the serve;
2. the ball bounces twice in the opponents' half;
3. an opponent heads the ball into the net;

4. an opponent heads the ball over the playing field boundary;
5. an opponent does not hit the ball with the head;
6. a player steps over the opponents' boundary.

Variations 1. Limit passing from unlimited to first-time passing. 2. The ball may be passed with the foot within the team, but it must be headed over the net. 3. The number of players can be changed, depending on the age and performance abilities of the players.

Comments The central circle is also suitable for a playing field. In practice, the game has proven especially worthwhile with lighter balls, such as volleyballs, rubber or plastic balls. Because of their greater elasticity in bouncing, greater demands are made on the reaction abilities of all participants. The game is suitable for advanced players and can be played indoors.

88   Heading Volleyball

Number of Players 2 teams with 6 to 8 players.

Playing Field 18 m x 9 m (volleyball court), divided on the halfway line by a net, 2. 4 m high .

Duration of Game 2 winning sets up to 20 points.

Objective of Game The ball must be hit into the opposing half with the head, and may not fall to the ground. Only the team serving can win a point.

Game Description A player begins in any position in his own half and heads the ball to the opponent. The ball may only be played directly, but can be headed to other players within the team four times. Heading the ball back does not have to be done in any particular order. Each team has five serves in a row, which must be made by different players each time. The serve follows every error. An error occurs whenever the ball:

1. touches the net in a serve;
2. lands outside of the field;
3. falls to the ground;
4. is headed within the team more than four times;
5. is not played with the head;
6. is not directly played by a player.

Variations 1. Head the serve over the net from behind one's own line.
2. Permit the ball to be played more often than four times. 3.
Each player must head the ball before it is hit over the net.

Comments Players must have a master of the basics of heading. The
game is suitable for advanced players and can be played
indoors.

89 Heading through Rings

Number of Players 2 teams with 4 to 6 players each.

Playing Field Gymnasium rings of approximately 1 m radius on ropes hanging from the ceiling, at least 1 m over the heads of the players.

Duration of Game Up to 30 min.

Objective of Game The team with the ball scores goals when a player succeeds in heading a ball through a ring. One point is awarded for a header through a ring from one's own hand; two points are for a hit scored directly from a throw.

Game Description Passing within a team follows from the hand.

All players may participate in scoring goals. The game is played without interruption and with barriers. After scoring, the team that wins possession of the ball continues playing.

Variations The game can be made more difficult by pulling the rings higher.

Comments Adjust the size of the rings to the abilities of the players but they must have a radius of at least 80 cm. This game can be played on a grass field if stands for the rings are available.

Throwing-in

114

90 Throw-in Game

Number of Players 2 teams of 5 players.

Playing Field 40 m x 20 m, 2 small field goals.

Duration of Game Up to 30 min.

Objective of Game Each team tries to attack the opponent's goal and score points through skillful positional play. The movement of the ball and the goals are made with regulation throw-ins.

Game Description One team begins the game. The ball may only be thrown with both hands above the head and both feet on the ground. The opponent gets possession of the ball if he wins it, if the ball goes out of play, or if the ball is passed with the foot. Corner balls are thrown in and the game is played without regular goalkeepers, and without offside.

Variations 1. Play with a throwing circle of approximately 10 m in radius. 2. Play with a large makeshift goal and a regular goalkeeper.

Comments This game is suitable for all age and performance groups. It can be played indoors with a correspondingly smaller playing field.

91 Hustle Ball

Number of Players 3 teams of 4 to 6 players.

Playing Field 30 m x 20 m, 3 fields, the middle field can be larger.

Duration of Game Up to 20 min.

Objective of Game Each team occupies a field. The players in the outer fields try to tag the players in the middle field. Only regulation throw-ins are valid tags.

Game Description The ball may be played no more than twice within one's own team. Only the teams in the outer fields have the right to throw out. Players in the middle field are not allowed to catch the ball. They can protect themselves from being tagged only through skillful evasion. The team in the middle trades places with one of the other teams after five throw-outs. The ball is returned to the players in the outer field after each hit.

Variations Play with several balls at the same time.

Comments In order to teach longer throw-ins, the playing field can be lengthened. The game can be played indoors.

92 Two Field Ball

Number of Players 2 teams of 6 to 8 players.

Playing Field 20 m x 10 m divided into 2 fields by a halfway line.

Duration of Game Up to 20 min.

Objective of Game Both teams occupy one field each and send one player behind the opponents' line. The team with the ball tries to pass the ball with throw-ins so that an opposing player can be tagged. The winner is the team which has tagged all the opposing players.

Game Description Players who are tagged must stand behind the opponents' line. The players behind the line have a permanent right to throw in and, if they tag someone, they can go back into the field. Players in the field have the right to throw in only if the ball is caught in their half. The ball changes if it is caught by the team without the ball during a throw-in.

Comments To teach long distance throw-ins, the playing field should be lengthened. To strengthen the muscles of the upper body, the game can be played with a medicine ball. The game is suitable for advanced performance and can be played indoors.

Tackling

Two Goal Game

93 Game in Two Fields

Number of Players 2 teams of 5 players.

Playing Field 40 m x 29 m; halfway line; an approximately 2 m wide goal on both long sides.

Duration of Game Up to 25 min.

Objective of Game Each team is divided into three attackers and two fullbacks. The attackers try to score goals and the fullbacks try to prevent them from doing so.

Game Description Three players from each team are in one half, and two in the other half of the playing field so that in each half, three always play against two to score a goal. Crossing the halfway line is not allowed. The attackers in the other field gain possession of the ball if the fullbacks win it, if it goes out of play, or if a rule is broken.

Variations Limit the passing of the attackers. Specify the number of times the ball may be touched as well as a time limit within which the attack must be completed.

Comments The players must exchange positions at regular intervals. This game is also suitable for smaller indoor fields in which the walls are used as barriers.

Drills and Games to Teach Tactics

Getting Free and Covering

Team Games

94   Two-on-Two in the Central Circle

Number of Players 2 teams of 2 players each.

Playing Field Central circle with halfway line.

Duration of Game At the edge of each half of the circle are two players who, by constantly getting free, make it possible for their teammates to pass.

Game Description The game begins with a low throw. The player who wins the ball can win a point if he succeeds in passing the ball through the circle so that his teammate on the other side can reach it. Entering the circle and crossing the halfway line outside of the circle are not allowed. The game is played without breaks. After three attempts, the player must pass. It is important for the teammate to get free on the other side. Hand signals are allowed.

Comments At first, the game can be played with the halfway line only. Later the distance can be extended to the size of a circle. This game is mainly for advanced players. It can be played indoors.

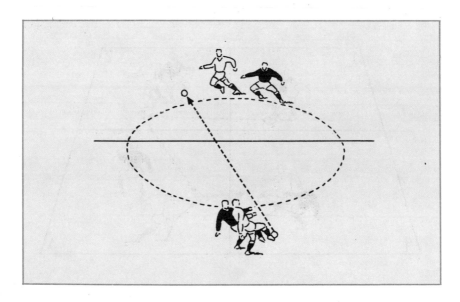

95 Team Ball in Four Fields

Number of Players 2 teams of 4 players.

Playing Field 20 m x 20 m, 4 equal fields.

Duration of Game Up to 20 min.

Objective of Game The fields are numbered. A player from each team is in each field. If a team succeeds in holding on to the ball and moving it in the field order 1-2-3-4, it wins a point.

Game Description Players must keep to their own fields. If a player wins the ball from the opposing team, the game continues in his field; and after three passes in a clockwise direction, this team also wins a point. The same happens if the opponent gets the ball when it goes into touch, if the boundary is crossed, or if there is a foul.

Variations Play without a specified direction: when the game is played in this way, a point is given for every pass.

Comments Bigger fields should be set up for less experienced players. The game is suitable for advanced players, in which case it can be played indoors.

96   Numbers Game

Number of Players 2 teams of 4 to 7 players.

Playing Field Half of the soccer field without goals.

Duration Of Game Up to 30 min.

Objective of Game Each team tries to pass the ball in a certain order to score goals.

Game Description Each team has different colour vests numbered sequentially. One team begins the game and can win a point, if it succeeds in passing the ball from player 1 to player 2 and on to player 3, and so on, through the whole team, without the opponents getting the ball. The ball may only be passed in sequential order. The opposing team gets the ball after every point won, when it wins the ball, when the ball goes out of play, or after a foul.

Variations 1. The player who wins the ball can immediately continue playing in the proper order, without first passing the ball back to player 1. 2. Limit the number of times the ball is touched from unlimited to first-time passing.

Comments Pairs of players are useful for practising covering: number 1 against number 1, number 2 against number 2, and so on, to prevent grouping around one player. The game is best suited for advanced players.

97   Game with Captains

Number of Players 2 teams of 4 to 6 players.

Playing Field Half of a soccer field.

Duration of Game Up to 30 min.

Objective of Game Each team chooses a captain. A team wins a point when it succeeds in passing the ball to its captain.

Game Description One team begins the game and tries to pass to its captain. The other team tries to prevent this, while at the same time it tries to win the ball. The team gains possession of the ball by winning it, when the ball goes out of play, or after the opponent scores. The captains change with another player after a certain time.

Variations The team that scores keeps the ball and continues playing.

Comments The captain of each team should be clearly recognizable (cap, sweat band, etc.) This game is suitable for advanced players.

98   Five-on-Five without a Goal

Number of Players 2 teams of 5 players.

Playing Field Half of the soccer field.

Duration of Game Up to 30 min.

Objective of Game The team with the ball must hold on to the ball as long as possible, and the other team must capture it. If a team succeeds in keeping the ball for one minute, it receives a point.

Game Description The players of one team begin by passing the ball to each other as long as possible. The opponent gets the ball only by capturing it, or whenever the ball goes out of play. If a point is won through good teamwork, the team may keep the ball and continue playing. High passing is allowed.

Variations 1. The point system can be changed according to the abilities of the team (for example, give a point for five first-time passes, for a long pass over 20 m, for possession of the ball over a longer or shorter period of time). 2. Two teams of three, four or six players with a corresponding playing field size (man-to-man marking).

Comments The fewer the players, the more difficult teamwork will be, and the more suited it is to advanced players.

Attacking

99   Game with One Goal

Number of Players 7 players, 4-on-3.

Playing Field Half of the soccer field.

Duration of Game Up to 30 min.

Objective of Game The three forwards must fight against four fullbacks, outplay or play around them, and shoot for the goal. The winner is the team that has scored the most points. The game is played without goalkeepers.

Game Description The forwards have the ball and begin their game outside the penalty area. If they succeed in shooting or heading the ball toward the goal, they get a point; if they score, they get two points. Only the shots made from within the penalty area are counted. If the defense captures the ball and dribbles it back over the halfway line, it wins a point. The forwards must try to capture the ball back.

Variations The roles are reversed every five minutes; one fullback then stays with the defense.

Comments This game is also possible with a ratio of five-on-four and six-on-five (suitable for advanced players).

100 Five-Minute Game

Number of Players 2 teams of 4 to 6 players and one regular goalkeeper.

Playing Field Half of the soccer field, one standard goal and halfway line.

Duration of Game By intervals, up to 6 x 5 min. per team.

Object of Game One team tries, by exploiting tactical variants, to attack the goal and score goals, while the other defends.

Game Description The goalkeeper begins the game with a neutral goal kick to the forwards, who are posted in the field behind the halfway line. They should shoot for goals by passing behind the backs of the defense, by skillful position change, by dribbling by the wing forwards, by shots in front of the defense, or by powerful combination play. After unsuccessful attacks, the game resumes in the attacker's half. For this, all forwards must have cleared the defending half. The team change should be made every five minutes.

Variations 1. Include defenders in the attack. 2. Specify other tactical variants.

Comments Put the teams together in such a way that they must play from their positions. The game is suitable for advanced players.

101 Deep Pass Game

Number of Players 2 teams of 4 to 6 players.

Playing Field Soccer field, halfway line.

Duration of Game Up to 30 min.

Objective of Game Both teams play on the half across from the goal. One team begins and tries to keep possession of the ball. The team is awarded one point for each minute it controls the ball. At a signal from the coach, a deep pass is made to a player of one's own team in the free field, and with that, the attack is set in motion. The goals resulting from the deep pass and the points for keeping the ball in the team determine the winner.

Game Description Before passing the ball into the free field, the halfway line may not be crossed. The opponents get the ball, if they win it, if a shot misses, or if the ball is lost. The game is played without offside, but with corner kicks.

Variations After an attack, the game continues in the same half, and the goalkeeper goes to the opposite goal.

Comments The game is suitable for advanced players. Weaker players play sideways across the soccer field into a makeshift goal.

102 The English Half

Number of Players 2 teams of 2 to 5 players and 1 neutral goalkeeper.

Playing Field Half of the soccer field with a standard goal.

Duration of Game Up to 60 min.

Objective of Game The team with the ball attacks to score goals. If the ball is lost it tries to prevent goals and to recapture the ball. Exploiting chances under pressure and — for the goalkeeper — positional play in 1-on-1 situations is decisive.

Game Description The goalkeeper begins the game with a neutral throw. The team that wins the ball, begins the game. The game is played according to FIFA rules, but without offside. After a goal is scored, the goalkeeper gets the ball and the game continues.

Variations A goal scored off a first-time pass can be given two points, a headed goal, three.

Comments This game is suitable for beginners as well as for advanced players.

103 Three Field Game

Number of Players 18 players, 8 on 8 with regular goalkeepers.

Playing Field A soccer field is divided into three — two 25 m areas and a middle area approximately 50 m wide and marked by two lines, each 25 m in front of the goal.

Duration of Game Up to 60 min.

Objective of Game One team attacks, the other defends its goal. The five forwards posted in midfield must overcome their five opposing players quickly to score.

Game Description The teams are divided up so that three fullbacks play in each 25 m field in front of their own goal, and five forwards play in midfield. The forwards can leave the middle field to attack the opponents' goal. The three fullbacks may not leave the 25 m zone and the forwards of their own team may not enter it. The game is played without offside, but with regular goalkeepers.

Variations The fullbacks trade places with three forwards after a certain time.

Comments Enlarge or reduce the attacking zone according to the abilities of the players. The game is suitable for advanced players.

104 Game with Three Zones

Number of Players 3 teams of 3 to 5 players.

Playing Field Half of a soccer field, 2 small field goals and halfway line.

Duration of Game Up to 60 minutes.

Objective of Game One team attacks a goal to score, while the other teams defend the goal and try to win the ball.

Game Description The team with the ball may attack a goal until it scores or loses the ball. If the ball is lost, the team takes over the goal it had just been attacking, while the team with the ball attacks the goal on the other side. The team in front of the goal may not go over the halfway line. The last player of each team in front of the goal may play the ball with his hands. There are no offsides.

Variations 1. Teams with a larger number of players can play on standard goals. 2. Vary the method of kicking for the shot.

Comments Adjust the stress endurance to the abilities of the players.

105 Numbers Game with Goal Shot

Number of Players 2 teams of 3 to 5 players.

Playing Field 40 m x 20 m, 2 small field goals.

Duration of Game Until all players of one team have scored a goal.

Objective of Game The players of both teams are given a number. Each player must score a goal according to a previously specified order.

Game Description One team begins and tries to get its player 1 free until he has scored. After this, player 2 must do the same, and so on. The opponent gets the ball by winning it, if it goes out of play, and after corner kicks and fouls. The game is played without a regular goalkeeper. The last player in front of the goal may hold the ball with his hands. There are no offsides.

Variations 1. Limit number of times a ball may be touched. 2. Designate the playing foot for the shot beforehand.

Comments This game is suitable for advanced teams.

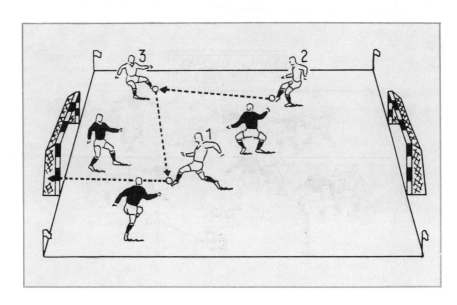

106   Shooting Game with Two Goals

Number of Players 14 players, 6-on-6, 2 regular goalkeepers.

Playing Field Double penalty area.

Duration of Game Up to 30 min.

Objective of Game One team attacks to score goals, while the defenders try to end the attack and win the ball.

Game Description The fullbacks of both teams may not cross the halfway line. They are included in the offensive play, being allowed to shoot the ball at the opponents' goal from their half. The forwards, as well, may play only in the opposing half, so that three always play against three in each half. A free-kick is given from the penalty area line if a rule is broken. The game is played with offside. Passing the ball from the forward to the fullback over the halfway line is permitted.

Variations 1. To support the forwards, one fullback from each team can be allowed to cross the halfway line. 2. Change the playing field, possibly enlarging the penalty area to 20 m (the playing field will then be 40 m).

Comments The game is suitable for advanced players.

107 Three-on-Two with a Goal

Number of Players 2 teams of 5 players, 2 regular goalkeepers.

Playing Field Regular soccer field.

Duration of Game Up to 30 min.

Objective of Game Both teams divide up their players so that in each half three forwards play against two fullbacks. Each team has a regular goalkeeper. The forwards must pass the ball so that they can shoot at the goal without pressure. The fullbacks try to win the ball and pass it to their forwards.

Game Description The halfway line can be passed, but players may not cross. The game changes to the other side after a goal, after a ball goes out of play, or if the ball has been won. The goalkeeper can pass the ball to his fullbacks or immediately to the forwards. No offsides.

Variations 1. Vary the combinations: four players against three, and five against four. 2. Play sideways over half the soccer field, using two small field goals without regular goalkeepers.

Comments The game is suitable for advance players.

108 Wing Game

Number of Players 2 teams of 7 to 11 players.

Playing Field Soccer field; mark an 8 m to 12 m wide outer goal in front of the standard goal.

Duration of Game Up to 40 min.

Objective of Game The attacking team must play the ball through the outer goal before it may shoot at the standard goal.

Game Description Attacks are only valid, if they go through the outer goal in the opposing half. There are two possibilities for this: either the player can dribble the ball through the outer goal or the ball may be passed through the outer goal and taken over by an inside forward. In both cases, the attack is valid and can be completed with a shot.

Variations Teams with fewer players play sideways across half of the soccer field. Set up the outer goals correspondingly.

Comments The width of the outer goal depends on the abilities of the teams. The better the players, the smaller the outer goal can be. The game is suitable for advanced players.

109 Game with Barriers

Number of Players 2 teams of 3 to 5 players.

Playing Field Indoors.

Duration Of Game Up to 2 x 30 min.

Objective of Game The game is played like hockey. There are no throw-ins and corner kicks. To teach double passes, the game is played on the long side and end wall of the gymnasium until a goal is scored.

Game Description The game begins like a normal soccer game. By including the barrier and excluding throw-ins and corner kicks, this game not only teaches double passing, but also increases demands on the players' fitness.

Variations A bonus point can be given for a double pass on the barrier that results in a completed goal.

Comments Gymnastic benches can be used as barriers.

110 Five Goal Game

Purpose Game movement (endurance and shooting accuracy).

Number of Players 2 teams of 5 to 8 players.

Playing Field Soccer field with five 2 m wide goals placed lengthways.

Duration of Game Up to 60 min.

Objective of Game Both teams play into five goals. Through rapid game movement, three points can be scored on the outer goals, two points on the second goals, and one point on the middle goal.

Game Description The game is played according to FIFA rules. The standard goals are set out of the way. The game is played without offside and corners. After every scored goal (point) the opponent gets the ball and can continue playing. Goals can be scored from both sides.

Variations 1. The width and distance of the goals can be changed. 2. The method of a shot can be specified (inside of the foot, outside of the foot, and instep).

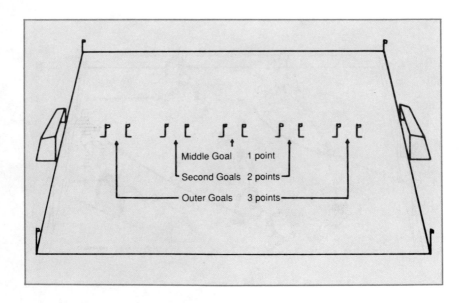

Middle Goal 1 point
Second Goals 2 points
Outer Goals 3 points

111 Counter Game with Wingers

Purpose Teaching rapid game set up.

Number of Players 5 forwards against 5 defenders and one neutral goalkeeper.

Playing Field Half the soccer field, with a standard goal and a 4 m wide side goal on the halfway line.

Duration of Game Up to 10 goals.

Objective of Game The forwards begin the attack from the halfway line according to FIFA rules. During the attack of the defenders on the outer goals, offside is removed. The defenders can score a goal if they win the ball and play it through one of the outer goals in three moves (dribbling is considered a move).

Variations 1. The defenders must play without a goalkeeper. 2. The defenders can only score a goal if the ball is played into a side goal in two moves.

Comments The side goals can be made larger or smaller depending on the abilities of the players.

Defending

140

112 Offside Half

Purpose Teaching offside tactics.

Number of Players 2 teams of 4 to 6 players, 1 regular goalkeeper.

Playing Field Half of the soccer field, 1 standard goal.

Duration of Game Up to 60 min.

Objective of Game One team attacks from the halfway line to score goals, while the other team tries to force the forwards offside through skillful defensive play. The forwards get a point for every goal, the fullbacks for every successful offside play.

Game Description If the fullbacks capture the ball, the forwards must begin the attack again. The offside manoeuvres of the fullbacks follow according to the game situation. The game can be played with man-to-man marking, zone defense, or combined defense.

Variations 1. After a certain time, both teams change roles. 2. Vary the number of players for the attack of the defense.

Comments Be clear about the offside rules prior to the game.

113 Man-to-Man

Purpose Teaching man-to-man marking.

Number of Players 2 teams of 4 to 8 players.

Playing Field Half of the soccer field with halfway line, 2 small field goals.

Duration of Game Up to 30 min.

Objective of Game The forwards of one team play in the opposing half, to score goals, while the fullbacks try to prevent goals with close man-to-man marking.

Game Description The game begins with the fullbacks passing the ball over the halfway line to the forwards. These are each personally guarded by a fullback. The fullbacks may only tackle their own personal opponent. Assisting teammates is not allowed. The opponent gets the ball if the fullbacks win it, after goals, balls going out of play, or after fouls. The game is played without goalkeepers and without offsides. The halfway line may not be crossed by the individual groups. Handling the ball is forbidden.

Variations The game is played with goalkeepers and the fullbacks may participate in shooting for a goal.

Comments This game is especially suitable for advanced teams.

114 Two-Times-Three Goal Game

Purpose Teaching securing the goal.

Number of Players 2 teams of 3 players.

Playing Field Half of a soccer field, mark 3 makeshift goals in each half (with flags etc.).

Duration of Game Up to 60 min.

Objective of Game One team attacks the opponents' half in order to score a goal from whichever side of the three-sided goal it chooses, while one opposing player guards each side of the goal to prevent scoring.

Game Description A goal is scored if the ball has crossed one of the three goal lines. A shot may only come from the opposing half. Each player is personally responsible for a goal line and teammates may not help him if his goal line remains unguarded. The opponent gets the ball by winning it, if the ball goes out of play, after a foul, or after goals.

Variations 1. Handling the ball is not permitted. 2. All players may help secure all goal lines.

Comments The size of the goals and the duration of stress must be adjusted according to the abilities of the players (game suitable for advanced players).

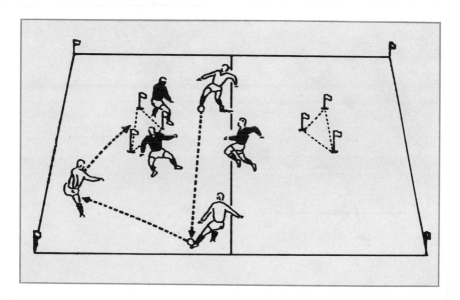

143

Position Training

Two Goal Game

115 Positional Play in Three Fields

Purpose Teaching positional play.

Number of Players 2 teams of 9 to 11 players.

Playing Field Soccer field, 3 equal fields.

Duration of Game Up to 40 min.

Objective of Game All participants play in their positions. In front of each of the two goals are three forwards against three fullbacks. Three runners from each team are in midfield. A team attacks to score goals by passing the ball from one field to the next, and defends its own goal when the opponent attacks.

Game Description The field boundaries may not be crossed. The game is begun by the fullbacks of one team who pass the ball to their teammates in midfield and in the opponents' field. From midfield, the ball may only be passed to the forwards. The last man of each team acts as goalkeeper and may handle the ball in the penalty area. There are no offsides.

Variations 1. Passing over the midfield is allowed. 2. Divide up the positions according to all tactical variants like 4-3-3, 4-2-4, and so on.

Comments The use of regular goalkeepers will ensure competitive training. The game is suitable for advanced player.

Drills and Games for Supplementary Training

116 Simplified Basketball

Purpose Psychological relaxation.

Number of Players 2 teams of 5 players.

Playing Field 26 m x 14 m, 3.05 m basket with backboard 4.6 m behind the free throw line, central circle.

Duration of Game Up to 40 minutes.

Objective of Game To score, one team tries to throw the ball in the basket defended by the opponent. If the ball is lost, the team defends its own basket.

Game Description Do not to play the game exactly according to basketball rules. Play according to gymnasium handball rules in field play. Note the following: 1. The face-off follows a high throw. 2. Foul play in the attacking half is penalized with a direct free throw for the basket. The player who has been fouled must make the throw. 3. A successful throw during the game is worth two points, while only one point can be scored with a free throw.

Variations 1. Increase or reduce the number of players. 2. Limit movement of the ball to first-time passing.

Comments No physical contact is permitted.

117 Handball Game

Purpose Psychological relaxation.

Number of Players 2 teams with 7 players each.

Playing Field 10 m x 20 m, throwing circle 2 m in radius in front of both small field goals.

Duration of Game Up to 60 min.

Objective of Game Both teams try to throw the ball in the opposing goal and to protect their own goal.

Game Rules Playing is done only with the hands. The rules forbid:

1. taking more than three steps while holding the ball;
2. stepping into the throwing circle;
3. obstructing the opponent by unfair means (holding, hitting the ball, pushing, etc.)

Breaking the rules is penalized by a free throw and, in serious cases, with a 7 m ball. For our purposes, the movement of the ball can follow handball rules.

Variations 1. Limit ball movement to first-time passing. 2. Increase or reduce number of players.

Comments To make the game more fun, play with a rugby ball.

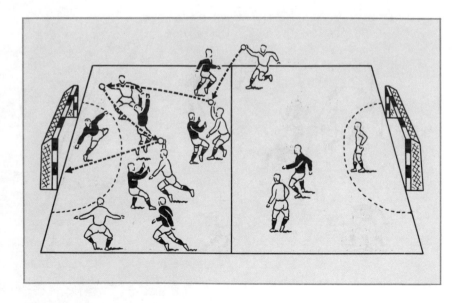

118 Team Ball Using a Medicine Ball

Purpose Psychological relaxation.

Number of Players 2 teams of 4 to 6 players.

Playing Field 40 m x 20 m without goals.

Duration of Game Up to 30 min.

Objective of Game Each team must hold on to the ball to collect points. A point is given for each first-time pass.

Game Description The game is played with the hands only and with first-time passing. The opponent gets the ball by capturing it, or if it goes into touch. It is useful to have two referees to monitor the action of each team and keep scores.

Variations 1. Change the scoring: for example, a point for five direct passes or for holding on to the ball for over a minute. 2. Vary the passing: for example, only with the right or left hand, letting the ball bounce once, only low, backwards, over the head, or through straddled legs.

119 Fist Tennis

Purpose Psychological relaxation.

Number of Players 1-on-1.

Playing Field 8 m x 4 m, a bench or medicine ball as halfway line.

Duration of Game 2 winning sets up to 21 points.

Objective of Game Exactly as in table tennis, but with a soccer ball (volleyball, rubber ball) and the fist as a paddle. The ball must be hit into the opponent's half and, after it has touched the ground once, hit back over the net. The player who wins 21 points first is the game winner. The winner is the player who wins two games. In a tie-breaker, sides are changed after 10 points in the third set.

Game Description Each player has five serves alternately. The serve follows each error behind a player's boundary. An error occurs whenever the ball:
1. touches the net during a serve;
2. lands outside the field;
3. bounces more than once;
4. is not hit with the fist.

Variations Play doubles (2-on-2).

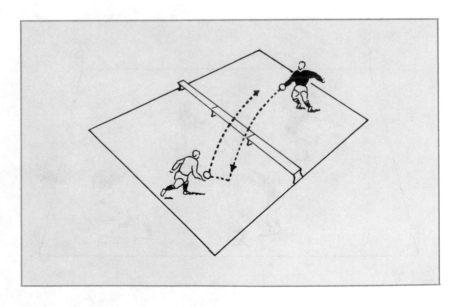

120 Volleyball

Purpose Psychological relaxation.

Number of Players 2 teams of 6 players.

Playing Field Volleyball court, 1 net 2.4 m high.

Duration of Game 2 winning sets, up to 15 points.

Objective of Game Each team must put the ball over the net into the opponents' half with the hands and try, in its own field, not to let the ball touch the ground to prevent scoring. A point can be scored only when the team is in possession of the ball.

Game Rules The serve begins the game and takes place again after every error behind one's own line, at which time the players change places clockwise in numerical order. In a field game, at least every third ball must go over the net. If the team with the ball commits an error, the serve changes to the opposing side. An error occurs whenever the ball touches the ground, lands outside of the field, is played by one player twice in a row, is hit with a part of the body under the waist, or is held or caught. In addition, the net must not be touched, and the opponents' half may not be entered.

Comments The height of the net and the number of players can be changed.

121 Earth Ball Game

Purpose Psychological relaxation.

Number of Players 2 teams of 3 to 5 players.

Playing Field According to the size of the gymnasium, from 15 m x 10 m upwards, 2 small field goals.

Duration of Game Up to 20 min.

Objective of Game The game is played with sticks approximately 40 cm long, made of old broom or shovel handles and a ball (tennis ball or rubber ball). Both teams try to put the ball over the opponents' goal line with their sticks, and try to prevent shots on their own goal.

Game Description The game begins like ice hockey with a face-off. The ball may only be played or hit with the stick. Hitting with the hand or foot is not allowed. Only the goalkeeper may hold the ball with his hand. For shooting, he must also use the stick. Infractions are penalized with a free hit.

Variations 1. The last man of every team is the goalkeeper. 2. Play with a shooting circle.

122 Rowdy Ball

Purpose Psychological relaxation.

Number of Players 2 teams of 5 to 8 players.

Playing Field 30 m x 15 m.

Duration of Game Up to 20 min.

Objective of Game The ball may be thrown, rolled, or carried. Using the feet is not allowed. Only balls placed behind the opponents' line count as goals. If the ball is rolled or thrown over the line, the opponent gets a free throw from where the ball lands. A free throw is also given if the ball goes out of play, or with a foul. The player with the ball may be obstructed or held, but not kicked or pushed. Blind spot situations (pile-ups) are settled with a high ball.

Variations 1. Play with makeshift goals only 4 m wide. 2. Allow playing with the foot as well.

Comments In this fighting game, pay particular attention to fair play. Roughness should be penalized initially by removing the player from the game off for a time, later with suspension.

123 Ringette

Purpose Psychological relaxation.

Number of Players 2 teams of 5 to 8 players.

Playing Field Depending on the size of the gymnasium, 15 m x 10 m upwards, 2 makeshift goals, 2 m wide.

Duration of Game Up to 40 min.

Objective of Game All players have gymnastic sticks. The attacking team tries to score by flinging a rubber ring into the opponents' goal and preventing scoring on its own goal.

Game Description The ring may be played only with the stick. Scoring is possible from both sides of the makeshift goals. The game is played with barriers and without touch balls. Free kicks are given to the opponent for pushing or charging, hitting with the stick, or playing the ring with the foot. The goalkeeper may stop the ring with his foot. If more than two players have their poles in the ring, a face-off takes place at this point.

Variations Use a throwing circle with a radius of approximately 4 m, which the players in the field may not enter.

124 Simplified Field Hockey

Purpose Psychological relaxation.

Number of Players 2 teams of 11 players.

Playing Field 91 m x 50 m, 2 small field goals, with 14. 6 m large shooting circles in front of them.

Duration of Game Up to 70 min.

Objective of Game The game is played with field hockey sticks (bent at the bottom and flattened on the left side) and a ball. Both teams try to hit the ball into the opposing goal with the flat side of the stick. If possession of the ball is lost, the roles of the two teams are reversed.

Game Description As a supplement to soccer training, it is useful in this form of hockey not to play exactly according to the rules and not on a regular field. The following should be noted:

1. A goal can only be scored in the opponents' shooting circle.
2. To begin the game, at halftime, after goals, and in contentious cases, the game continues with a face-off.
3. Free hits are given for foul play in midfield (charging, stopping the ball with the body, touching the ball with the round side of the stick, and lifting the stick over shoulder height).

4. Penalty face-offs are given for fouls in the shooting circle 4. 5 m in front of the middle of the opponents' goal.
5. Balls going out of play are rolled in.
6. The ball can be stopped with the stick, with the hand, or caught.However,it must come to a stop or fall straight down.
7. No offsides are called. Corners and penalty corners are played.

Variations Have fewer players and the same size shooting circle sideways across half of the soccer field.

Comments This game can also be played six players against six in a gymnasium if the room is at least 40 m x 20 m.

Coaching Tips on How to Use the Drills and Games

All drills and games contained in this book are of a complex character. The main elements of soccer — fitness, techniques, tactics — are so intertwined that keeping them distinct is difficult. Therfore although an attempt has been made to organize the games according to their main characteristics, the organization adopted in this book has resulted in some overlapping of games. For example, the game "Five-on-Three" (Game 25) is placed in the section on endurance training; but in this game the larger group of players is also trained in tactics (getting free covering) and technique (passing). The smaller group of players must, at the same time, develop peripheral vision as well as dribbling and tackling skills (see the analysis in the Table below).

Coaches or instructors can analyze each drill similarly and decide for themselves how to use it within the framework of the main objective of the training session.

Table A sample analysis of Drill 25.

Number and Name of Game	endurance	speed	agility	inside of the foot kick	instep kick	inner instep kick	dribbling	heading	throw-in	tackling getting free	covering	attacking	defense	position training	psychological relaxation
25 Five- On-Three	0	—	—	X	—	—	X	—	—	X	X	—	—	X	—

Establishing the objectives for each training session and determining which drills and games meet those objectives is one of the most important responsibilities of a coach.